The Transformation of the Board of Trade
1830-1855

The enormous growth of industry and towns in early nineteenth-century Britain brought constant demands for Government action in the interests of public welfare and safety. However much *laissez-faire* was advocated as a theory, state intervention was becoming an established system, with the Board of Trade as its chief adminstrative agency.

The Board regulated the railways and the carriage of mails. It undertook the superintendence of the British merchant marine and concerned itself with the welfare of seamen. It set up the Meteorological Office. It was charged with the collection and publication of official statistics, and was responsible for the registration of joint stock companies. It organized schools of industrial design.

At the beginning of the century the Board had been an advisory committee of the old Privy Council for all matters of trade and foreign plantations. By 1855 it had been transformed into an executive department of state, and had become, in effect, a Board of Industry.

This study is important both as a history of the Board of Trade during a formative period and as a contribution to the neglected field of nineteenth-century administrative history.

THE TRANSFORMATION
OF THE
BOARD OF TRADE
1830 - 1855

A STUDY OF ADMINISTRATIVE REORGANIZATION
IN THE HEYDAY OF LAISSEZ FAIRE

by

ROGER PROUTY

WILLIAM HEINEMANN LTD
LONDON · MELBOURNE · TORONTO

FIRST PUBLISHED 1957

PUBLISHED BY
WILLIAM HEINEMANN LTD
99 GREAT RUSSELL STREET LONDON WCI

PRINTED BY THE WHITEFRIARS PRESS LTD
LONDON AND TONBRIDGE

" What was the Board of Trade for, if not to undertake the management of such matters as this? "

JOSEPH HUME in Parliament, 1836

PREFACE

IN the course of writing this book, which is based largely on Parliamentary Papers, it became clear that there was not only the well-known railway interest, but also the similarly organized shipping interest, whose evidence before Parliamentary inquiries is untrustworthy and sometimes dishonest. Behind this account of the development of the Board of Trade, there lies the as yet untold story of Parliamentary pressure groups, which I hope will be the subject of historical analysis in the future.

I wish to acknowledge the help of the officers of the Libraries of Columbia University, Harvard University, University of London, the Board of Trade, the Admiralty, and the Ministry of Transport and Civil Aviation, and of the Public Record Office and the Boston Athenaeum. The extracts from Hansard are reproduced by permission of Her Majesty's Stationery Office.

I am particularly indebted to Professor J. B. Brebner of Columbia University, who suggested the subject of this study and has given me continuous encouragement. I am also very much indebted to Mr. O. R. McGregor of Bedford College, University of London, who was of great help in preparing this manuscript for publication; and to Mr. H. L. Beales of the London School of Economics, University of London, and to Professor R. K. Webb of Columbia University.

These men have suggested lines of inquiry and have helped in the removal of errors, but they are in no way responsible for any errors which remain or for any opinions expressed.

Massachusetts Institute of Technology   ROGER PROUTY
June 1956

CONTENTS

CONTENTS

Legislation for Laissez Faire and Railways

INTRODUCTION

LAISSEZ faire in early nineteenth-century Britain was never a system. The textbook accounts of a government concentrating on the removal of all restraints and regulations on industry perpetuate a myth which is no longer acceptable. In a society fast industrializing and urbanizing, the demands made upon the Government to act in the general interest and in the interests of public welfare and safety grew more constant. While laissez faire as a general principle or as an argument against a particular measure might continue to receive wide publicity, it was persistently defeated in practice. Public safety forced Parliament to legislate for the carriage of troops and police on the railways, public convenience forced it to legislate for the carriage of mails, and public welfare required the Government's assistance in the disposal of sewage. The most determined liberal could not consistently argue for laissez faire; he sooner or later found himself advocating a measure which involved the Government in the regulation of some part of industry. State intervention may not have been policy but it was the growing reality.

But it was not only legislation for the public welfare which subverted laissez faire, it was also the legislation designed for its economic fulfilment. To many business men it necessitated legislation for economic freedom. It did not mean the removal of government but instead the persistence of government as the agent in the removal of traditional regulations in industry and in the maintenance of regulations which would ensure the free competition that would facilitate capitalist enterprise. The Government must act, in other words, to free production and distribution or trade, to free capital and labour; and it must continue to act to keep them free so that individual business men might compete on equal terms. Thus in freeing capital and facilitating the use of joint stock funds and in limiting the liability of investors the Government had to set up machinery for the regulation of companies using such funds both in the interests of public welfare and competition. And in freeing labour it replaced the old system of out-door relief, which discouraged the mobility of labour and allowed unemployment, with the Poor Law of 1834 which provided for the relief of the poor only in workhouses which offered a living less attractive than the least attractive living outside the workhouse walls. The unemployed had to move and find work or retreat to the miserable workhouses. Thus in getting a freer supply of labour, business men forced the Government to operate the workhouses.[1] The general application of laissez faire was impossible in an industrializing society; while the economic application required state intervention.

Historians have only recently begun to reappraise the meaning of laissez faire during the second quarter of the nineteenth century. J. B. Brebner in his article " Laissez Faire and State Intervention in Nineteenth-Century Britain " and K. Polanyi in *Origins of Our Time* emphasized the new interpretation.[2] Since then L. Robbins in *The Theory of Economic Policy* has explored the interventionism of the classical economists. E. Lipson in *The Growth of English Society* emphasized that it was in the eighteenth century when laissez faire received its fullest expression. Others have studied particular aspects of interventionism : M. W. Thomas in *The Early Factory Legislation*, S. E. Finer in *The Life and Times of Edwin Chadwick*, and R. A. Lewis in *Edwin Chadwick and the Public Health Movement 1832–1854*. Other briefer detailed accounts have been published by L. R. Sorenson and K. O. Walker in their articles, " Some Classical Economists, Laissez Faire, and the Factory Acts," and " The Classical Economists and the Factory Acts." This bibliography of the growth of government during the three decades before 1854 will continue to expand, especially since Civil Service reform before that date is now beginning to receive attention.

The growth of intervention required the growth of government. New boards and commissions such as the Poor Law Commission and the General Board of Health were created to perform certain duties. Some of these agencies have been examined in the histories already mentioned. But many other duties were given to the older branches of the Government, and with the exception of the Post Office, whose growth and reform during this period has been well set forth by H. Robinson in *The British Post Office*, no department or branch of the Government has received full attention.[3] Histories of individual departments are far too cursory in their accounts of this period. Furthermore the department that was most transformed and has received the least attention was the Board of Trade.

This department had already lost its responsibilities for the colonies to the Colonial Office early in the century; in the forties, with the victory of free trade, it lost its other chief hereditary duty. Yet the Board itself did not wither away because the Government found it the most convenient depository for many new jobs: it collected and published official statistics, it registered joint stock companies, it administered the schools of design, and it became generally responsible for the regulation of the two great transportation industries, railways and merchant shipping. In 1854 the Northcote-Trevelyan report on Civil Service reform summarized the recent history of the Board.

> There is probably no department of the Government to whose functions so many and such important additions have recently been made, as the Board of Trade. While, however, these additions have been of such a nature as almost entirely to change the character of the Department, its constitution has not yet been revised with a view to the efficient discharge of its new duties. Originally designed for consultative purposes, it was organized in a very different manner from the executive offices; and the arrangements made for the transaction of its business have not been such as are suitable to the management of administrative details.
>
> Of late years, however, a large amount of executive business, very important and very various in its nature, has been assigned to this Department. Thus in 1832 it was charged with the duty of collecting and publishing statistical information; since 1840 it has exercised a more or less minute control over the Railway Companies; about the same time the Government School of Design was placed under its superintendence; the Office for the Registration of Designs, and that for the Registration of Joint Stock Companies, have also been attached to it; and

within the last two years a new and most important addition
has been made to its functions by the Acts for the Regulation of
Merchant Shipping of the country, for the winding up and
determination of the Merchant Seamen's Fund, and for the
inspection of our Steam Navigation.

As each of these subjects has been successively assigned to the
Board of Trade, some provision has been made for supplying
the machinery required to deal with it : but this has generally
been done by adding to the Department either some new officer,
or some subordinate Board, specially charged with the management of the new business, and not by any such general recasting
of the office as would render it efficient as a whole for the dis-
charge of all its functions.[4]

The Board in fact was transformed from an advisory committee
of the Privy Council into an administrative department of state.

No history of this transformation has been written. The only
general history of the Board, that in the Whitehall Series by Sir
Hubert Llewellyn Smith, is far too brief; and all period histories
of the Board stop before 1820.[5] Biographies of the men at the
Board of Trade are all unsatisfactory because they fail to describe
the man's actual work at the Board. Yet there are good accounts
of certain of the Board's activities, particularly of its leadership
of the campaigns for freer trade and freer capital, and of its
attempts to regulate the railways. Although these histories were
not written to explain the nature of the transformation of the
Board, they do cover the subject so thoroughly that a full account
here would be repetitious. Therefore in this history only a brief
review of the Board's role in respect to these activities will be
offered. But since there is no satisfactory account of the Board's
administration of the schools of design, one chapter is devoted to
that particular responsibility. However, it is with the great
merchant shipping industry that this history is primarily concerned. Not only has no good account been published of the
Government's regulation of the industry during this period, but
it was this history which, far more than all the other activities
combined, really accounts for the Board's transformation.

It was a long and difficult task for the Government to work out
the regulations governing this vast industry. There were so many
different activities, almost independent one from another, that

each had to be treated separately. And it was only after long experimentation that Parliament realized that the responsibility for carrying out the regulations could not be distributed among nine departments but should be vested in the Board of Trade. Chapter III of this history describes the regulations that were worked out for each activity. Chapter IV then carries on the story from 1850 to 1854 when the Government came to realize that consolidation of the whole legal code was desirable and that the Board of Trade should assume responsibility for its operation. The great Merchant Shipping Act of 1854 not only clarified and defined the relations between the Government and merchant shipping, it also recognized the Board of Trade as an administrative department of state. In denying the myth of laissez faire it affirmed the transformation of the Board of Trade.

Before describing the Board's administration of the schools of design and its regulation of merchant shipping, it is necessary to review its role in legislation for laissez faire, for freer trade and capital, its office of official statistician, and its relationship to the railway industry.

FREE TRADE

The campaign for external free trade was long, for the old prejudice in favour of protection died hard.[6] It was only when the entrepreneurs associated with a particular industry became confident that they could undersell foreigners in a free market, that they became free traders. By the seventeen eighties men in certain industries such as cotton manufacturing were ready for free competition. Also by this time politicians realized that lowered duties on trade, carefully collected, would yield more revenue than the prohibitive duties which encouraged smuggling. Thus entrepreneurial confidence together with administrative reform resulted in William Pitt's famous reciprocal trade treaties, notably that with France in 1786. But this start in the direction of freer trade was soon halted by the outbreak of war in 1792. For the next thirty years prohibition and smuggling remained the order of the day.

Although the war was over in 1815, it took a few years for entrepreneurs and politicians to recover from the abnormal conditions and to become once again interested in reform. In 1820 a group of prominent London merchants presented a petition in favour of free trade to Parliament. The resulting committees of inquiry of both houses recommended many modifications in the old tariff structure. Meanwhile the officers of the Board of Trade had started the tremendous job of recodification of the two thousand statutes dictating customs duties. Before they could argue for reduced duties or reciprocal treaties with other countries, the reformers had to know what the old regulations were. The initiative was taken by the President of the Board of Trade, Frederick Robinson and his very able Vice-President, Thomas Wallace.[7] As chairman of the House of Commons committee of inquiry the latter supported the cause of freer trade with great industry and ability. But the job was only begun when William Huskisson became President of the Board in 1823.[8] Although all presidents and chief officers of the Board during these decades were men of ability, Huskisson was perhaps the ablest of all. A confirmed free trader, he pushed ahead vigorously with the work. James Deacon Hume, one of those dedicated men so useful during the age of reform, was his valued assistant.[9] In 1825, Huskisson was able to lay before Parliament ten bills which incorporated the new mercantile code, rewritten and simplified. With Parliament's acceptance of the new code, the next task, the general reduction of duties, could be continued methodically. During the next twenty years the duties on one item after another were lowered. Some reductions like those on timber from the Baltic required wide publicity and long debates in Parliament, but many others received hardly any notice. Meanwhile the Foreign Office and the Board of Trade were able to send men like John Macgregor abroad to negotiate reciprocal trade treaties.[10] Acting in their advisory capacity, the officers of the Board of Trade, who were all free traders, pushed the work forward year after year.

The Parliamentary inquiry of 1840 in reporting strongly for freer trade, prophesied its victory. By 1845 duties were retained not to control trade but only for revenue and therefore the Board of Trade undertook the revision of the tariff for the last time. Thereafter it became the responsibility of the Treasury. Having already surrendered the administration of the colonies to the Colonial Office, the Board had now legislated away its other historic responsibility.

FREER CAPITAL

While labour was made mobile and trade was freed, capital had to be made more available. The monopoly of the Bank of England was broken and the interest rate was freed, but more important still, capitalization by joint stock fund had to be facilitated. The traditional organization of business by partnership was clearly inadequate in this period when large sums of capital had to be raised and when more and more persons had small sums to invest in industry. Whereas the use of a joint stock fund had formerly been granted only as a privilege in a few cases, it now was made the right of all. Ownership and management no longer were necessarily identical. Now one or more persons could form a company or corporation, and after registering with the Board of Trade and meeting certain requirements, could sell stock to the public. And in the fifties Parliament limited the liability of investors to the amount of their stock. This history of the freeing of capital and of the reforming of company law has been well told.[11]

The presidents of the Board of Trade had always advised the Government on the granting of charters of incorporation. They had also been among the first to understand the need for reform during the eighteen thirties. Committees of inquiry had studied various aspects of company law and finance but it was only when the inquiry of 1843 recommended that the Board of Trade should set up an office for the registration of joint stock companies and that it should enforce certain regulations specified in the bill the report outlined, that Parliament was ready to act. Twenty years of agitation by a group of dedicated reformers, among them some of the officers of the Board of Trade, particularly Poulett Thomson, President during the thirties, and W. E. Gladstone, Vice-President and President from 1841 to 1845, prepared Parliament for the appropriate bill.[12] The Joint Stock Companies Act of 1844 obviated the confusion and expense of many private bills, regularized and facilitated the financing of business.[13] Capitalization was democratized.

Although the Registrar remained responsible to the Board of Trade, the fees he collected made him financially independent of the Board. As his work was largely autonomous, it had little effect on the Board.[14]

STATISTICS

Another of the responsibilities which the Board acquired was the collection and annual publication of official statistics. In order to carry on administration and reform in the industrializing society, the Government had to have a continuous stream of information. To know conditions and to measure change, it had to have statistical data. One politician said that " accurate knowledge of the actual condition and prospects of Society is an object of great national importance not to be obtained without a careful collection and classification of Statistical Facts." [15] From facts the reformer should derive " those principles upon which the well-being of society depends." And once determined, the facts and principles must be made known for " publicity was the true corrective of corruption." [16] Facts proved the need for any reform. Henry Brougham, the most ubiquitous of all the early Victorians, summed up their value by saying that " there was hardly anything which might not be proved by . . . [facts]; that they could be used equally by both sides; that, in short, you could prove anything and everything by their assistance." [17]

Members of Parliament called for more and more statistical returns every year. These reports were prepared upon each occasion by the appropriate officer or department. With the increase in the number called for, the expense to the Government became considerable. Lord Auckland, the President of the Board of Trade, realized that there would be a great saving in time and money if his department prepared annual general returns. Auckland's suggestion was immediately accepted by the officers of the Treasury and they authorized him to establish a department.[18] He chose G. R. Porter, a statistician and assistant to the publisher, Charles Knight, to be superintendent of the new branch.[19] Porter and his three clerks set to work combing through the bulky 314 folio volumes of the sessional papers for the previous twelve years. For other statistics he wrote letters to appropriate authorities, such as chambers of commerce, the National Debt Office, and to lord mayors.[20]

Beginning the next year, Porter was able to publish annually his consolidated returns. He was given a permanent appointment at £600 a year, and his branch became an official department of the

Board of Trade. In 1838 his salary was raised to £800, and he was given two more clerks.

Yet ten years later he testified before a select committee of the House of Commons that his returns had not been wholly successful. Often Members called for special returns or else requested returns without first asking his department if it could furnish them. Thus considerable expense continued to be incurred in the other departments of government. Another difficulty resulted from the frequent indifference of those to whom the department sent questions and their failure to return answers. Then too, the publications of the department sometimes were late and were not suitable for the specific purpose or use of the Member because they were too voluminous and included too much miscellaneous data.[21]

Yet the statistical department continued to perform helpful service. Its personnel continued to increase slowly and its annual report to gain authority. In 1847 Porter was replaced by Albany Fonblanque, the former editor of the *Examiner*. At that time the *Economist* said that Porter's work had "contributed in no small degree to the rapid development of correct views of late years, by furnishing to the reasoner facts on which he could rely in support of true theories." [22]

Although the statistical branch remained an important department of the Board of Trade, its functioning was a matter of the routine collection, compilation and publication of facts. Once established upon a regularized basis, its history adds little to an explanation of the transformation of the Board.

RAILWAYS

The Board of Trade became involved in the attempts of the Government to regulate the railways. Because that history has also been well told, only a brief review will be offered here.[23]

With the development of efficient steam locomotion in the early thirties, railways became the crucial factor in industrial development. They were projected and built all over Britain. Their growth is the most dramatic chapter in the industrial revolution. Their importance was clear, but their monopolistic nature was not. It was assumed that competition would force railway proprietors to operate in the interests of the public. They would compete with turnpikes and canals and, like those proprietors, charge tolls for anyone using the line. However, it was soon apparent that railways were monopolies. They eliminated the competition of turnpikes and canals, and because it was uneconomic to operate two lines between the same two towns, one line alone offered the required service. Furthermore, the operator of the line had to run all trains on his line. He, in fact, had a monopoly. Because of the importance of railways and the fact that their proprietors controlled monopolies, many persons soon realized that the Government faced a unique problem of regulation. They had to be regulated not only as a public utility but also to safeguard free private enterprise.

In the provisions of the individual private acts authorizing each railway, Parliament tried to exercise some control. However, although details of construction and operation may have been specified, no department of the Government was responsible for forcing the proprietors to comply. Furthermore, the number of private bills presented annually between 1837 and 1846 increased from 21 to 550. Since each bill had to be examined by an individual select committee of each house and debated, Parliament did not have time to consider each bill; it had to reform its procedure. One line of reform was to put all the clauses which were common to private acts into public acts which meant that the size of private acts were reduced to those clauses unique to each railway. The officers of the Board of Trade took the initiative in this reform of private bill procedure.

But the problem of regulating a public utility remained. Parliament passed an act in 1838 providing that railways should carry the mails at rates and times suitable to the Post Office. In 1842 it passed a similar act for the carriage of troops and police. Meanwhile an act in 1840 gave the Board of Trade responsibility for the collection of railway statistics and for the inspection of railways. These duties were given to the statistical department. Porter was given £200 more a year, and a law and corresponding clerk who was able to handle the important correspondence with the railways, was also responsible for the interpretation of the private acts of incorporation and of the railways' bylaws. Inspectors were to be hired when necessary.[24] But the power of the railway lobbies and the prejudice against governmental intervention prevented effective control. However, the Board's inspections and publicity encouraged more responsible management. In 1844 the President of the Board introduced a bill to give the Board more power, but the powerful railway interests in Parliament amended it so that it accomplished little. The industry was already very large and extensive and Parliament remained uncertain about how to regulate this new industry. Peel, the Prime Minister, was convinced that for the security of his cabinet he could not support the bill. It did provide that every line should run one third-class train daily.

The same year, railway business increased so much that the railway board was separated from the statistical department and set up separately with the President or the Vice-President of the Board of Trade as senior member. Lord Dalhousie, the Vice-President, and a man of extraordinary industry and ability, assumed responsibility.[25] This board was to examine all petitions for railways and make preliminary reports to Parliament. But even with increased personnel and despite the ability of some of its members, the board failed to do its work satisfactorily, simply because there was too much of it. The railway boom of 1845 left the conscientious board, unable to cope with all the work, open to the criticism of everybody. Its reports were late, its proceedings secret and its recommendations objectionable to somebody. The railway proprietors resented interference and Parliament was jealous of the Board's powers. The next year this Board was dismissed and a Board of Railway Commissioners was appointed. The Commissioners were not responsible to the Board of Trade but directly to Parliament. However, the Board still had influence because the Commissioners' office was at the Board of Trade and the President of the Board was one of the most active commissioners.

The Government regulated railways only to the extent necessitated by public safety and welfare. During the years after 1846, with the end of the construction boom, the Commissioners had so little to do that by 1851 they were considered an extravagance and disbanded. Their responsibilities were once again given to the Board of Trade, despite the protest of the Board's President who preferred not to be bothered with railways. The Board had slightly more authority than before; it might postpone the opening of a railway for a month, it might prescribe certain details about the construction of a road, it was to carry out inspections and report to Parliament, and it was to examine the causes of accidents involving loss of life. Yet effective regulation was successfully staved off by the railways for another twenty years.

NOTES

1 See H. L. Beales, " The New Poor Law," *History*, XV (1931), 308-19.

2 For further information see: J. Bartlet Brebner, "Laissez Faire and State Intervention in Nineteenth-Century Britain," *Journal of Economic History*, Supplement VIII (1948), 59-73; S. E. Finer, *The Life and Times of Sir Edwin Chadwick* (London, 1952); John Maynard Keynes, *The End of Laissez-Faire* (London, 1926); R. A. Lewis, *Edwin Chadwick and the Public Health Movement 1832-54* (London, 1952); E. Lipson, *The Growth of English Society* (London, 1949); F. C. Mather, " The Railways, the Electric Telegraph and Public Order During the Chartist Period, 1837-48," *History*, XXXVIII (1953), 40-53; Karl Polanyi, *Origins of Our Time* (London, 1945); Lionel Robbins, *The Theory of Economic Policy* (London, 1952); Lloyd R. Sorenson, " Some Classical Economists, Laissez Faire, and the Factory Acts," *The Journal of Economic History*, XII (1952), 247-62; Maurice Walton Thomas, *The Early Factory Legislation* (Leigh-on-Sea, 1948); M. W. Thomas, " Origins of Administrative Centralization," *Current Legal Problems* (1950), 214-35; and Kenneth O. Walker, " The Classical Economists and the Factory Acts," *Journal of Economic History*, I (1941), 168-77.

3 Howard Robinson, *The British Post Office* (Princeton, 1948).

4 *Parliamentary Papers* (hereafter *P. P.*), 1854, XXVII.

5 The Board of Trade was established in 1694. It advised the Government on matters of trade and was largely responsible for the administration of the colonies. At the time of the Whig economical reforms of 1782, it was abolished. Colonial correspondence was given to the Home Office, which in turn gave it over during the Napoleonic wars to the Secretary for War who also became the Secretary for the Colonies. He remained the Secretary for War and the Colonies until the Crimean wars, when it became obvious that the two responsibilities should be divided. Meanwhile the Permanent Under-Secretary for the Colonies, who really carried the responsibility, was referred to as the Colonial Secretary. After the conclusion of the American war in 1783 and the revival of trade, the Government recognized the usefulness of a Board of Trade and therefore re-established it.

The only general history of the Board of Trade is Sir Hubert Llewellyn Smith, *The Board of Trade* (London, 1928). Some of the works which discuss the Board before 1820 or have some information are: *The Cambridge History of the British Empire*, I (Cambridge, 1929); Charles Badham, *The Life of James Deacon Hume* (London, 1859); A. H. Basye, *The Lords Commissioners of Trade and Plantations, Commonly Known as the Board of Trade, 1748-1782* (New Haven, 1925); Ralph Paul Bieber, *The Lords of Trade and Plantations, 1675-1696* (Philadelphia, 1919); Mary Patterson Clark, " The Board of Trade at Work," *The American Historical Review*, XVII (1912), 17-43; Oliver Morton Dickerson, *American Colonial Government, 1696-1765* (Cleveland, 1912); Francis Edwin Hyde, *Mr. Gladstone at the Board of*

Trade (London, 1934); Anna Lane Lingelbach, "The Inception of the British Board of Trade," *American Historical Review,* XXX (1925), 701-27; and "William Huskisson as President of the Board of Trade," *American Historical Review,* XLIII (1938), 759-74; G. Poulett Scrope, *Charles Lord Sydenham* (London, 1844); Adam Shortt, *Lord Sydenham* (Oxford, 1926); and Margaret Marion Spector, *The American Department of the British Government, 1768-1782* (New York, 1940).

6 The following studies are the most helpful to the student of the campaign for free trade: Alexander Brady, *William Huskisson and Liberal Reform* (Oxford, 1928); Lucy Brown, "The Board of Trade and the Tariff Problem, 1840-2," *The English Historical Review,* LXIII (1953), 394-421; J. H. Clapham, "The Last Years of the Navigation Acts," *The English Historical Review,* XXV (1910), 480-501 and 687-707; A. R. M. Lower, "From Huskisson to Peel: a Study in Mercantilism," *Essays in Modern English History* (Cambridge, Mass., n.d.); and Robert Livingston Schuyler, *The Fall of the Old Colonial System* (New York, 1945).

7 Robinson, Frederick (1782-1859), Chancellor of Exchequer, 1823-27; created Viscount Goderich, 1827; Prime Minister, 1827-28; created Earl of Ripon, 1833; President of the Board of Trade, 1841-43.

Wallace, Thomas (1768-1844), Vice-President of the Board of Trade, 1818-23; created baron 1828; in favour of freer trade; considered by David Ricardo as a man of great merit.

8 Huskisson, William (1770-1830), President of the Board of Trade, 1823-27; good friend of Canning; representing Liverpool after 1823, he was particularly interested in shipping and trade problems and in reducing tariffs. Not a good orator, he was handicapped by his cold nature and his tactlessness.

9 Hume, James Deacon (1774-1842), Joint-Secretary to Board of Trade, 1828-40; joint founder of the Political Economy Club; primarily responsible for consolidating all the customs code into the ten Acts of 1825; an able Civil Servant; wrote letters to the Press on socialism in thirties.

10 Macgregor, John (1797-1857), collected statistics in America in twenties; travelled for Board of Trade in thirties; Joint-Secretary of Board, 1840; M.P. for Glasgow, 1847; promoter of Royal British Bank, 1849; absconded shortly before it stopped payment.

11 This bibliography is large; however, the most useful works are: Colin A. Cooke, *Corporation, Trust and Company* (Manchester, 1950); George Heverton Evans, Jr., *British Corporation Finance 1775-1850* (Baltimore, 1936); Bishop Carleton Hunt, *The Development of the Business Corporation in England 1800-67* (Cambridge, Mass., 1936); and H. A. Shannon, "The Coming of General Limited Liability," *Economic History,* II (1931), 261-91; and "The First Five Thousand Limited Companies and Their Duration," 396-424.

12 Thomson, Poulett (1799-1841), Vice-President of the Board of Trade, 1830-4; President, 1834-9; created Baron Sydenham, 1840. He was trained in the trading business of his father with the Baltic and had lived there and in Germany for several years. He was a friend of Bentham and the political economists. Bentham assisted personally in his first election to Parliament in 1826. (The election cost £3,000.) He knew more of business than any other member of the Government. Representing Manchester, he was particularly assiduous in working for freer trade and for the business interests. He also worked for efficiency and economy in the business of the Government.

He was not well-liked by most of his contemporaries but he commanded their respect because of his knowledge of business and his conscientiousness.

Gladstone, William Ewart (1809-98), the famous Prime Minister, was Vice-President of the Board of Trade, 1841-43, and succeeded Ripon as President 1843-5. Under the tutelage of his Prime Minister and mentor, Sir Robert Peel, he learned a respect for the business of government which helped him achieve his later successes. He was a most conscientious officer at the Board.

13 7 & 8 Vict. c. 110.

14 Frederic Rogers was appointed registrar. He was to receive £600 a year, his assistant for Ireland, £200; his three clerks, £200 to £80; and he was to have one office keeper. Fees were to be charged for registration so that a staff of three clerks was not considered excessive. Board of Trade Papers I, 439 (hereafter referred to as BT.).

15 *Annals of the Statistical Society* (London, 1934), p. 11.

16 *Journal of the Statistical Society* I (London, 1839), p. 1, and " Statistics,' *Encyclopædia Britannica*, Vol. XX, 7th ed.

17 *Parliamentary Debates,* 3rd series (hereafter *Parl. Deb.*) CIV, 1332.

18 Eden, George (1784-1849), a son of William Eden who assisted the younger Pitt; succeeded as Baron Auckland; President of the Board of Trade, 1830-4; Governor-General of India, 1835-41; created Earl of Auckland, 1839. He was respected for his conscientious attendance in the House of Lords and for his common sense, but was considered dull.

19 Porter, George Richardson (1792-1852), an ardent student of political economy and of statistics; helped organize the statistical branch at the Board, 1832; became Joint-Secretary to the Board, 1841, and remained one of the most active members of the staff until his death.

20 The Board of Trade Papers include many outletters, but the replies from the many different sources questioned are missing.

21 Porter's evidence before the Select Committee on Miscellaneous Expenditure in 1848, *P. P.*, 1847-8, XVIII, Part I.

22 *Economist,* V (1847), 929.

23 The bibliography of railway history is very extensive. The most helpful history of the development of railways and their relation to the state is Edward Cleveland-Stevens, *English Railways : their Development and their Relation to the State* (London, 1915). A recent analysis of the legal and legislative aspects of railways is O. Cyprian Williams, *The Historical Development of Private Bill Procedure and Standing Orders in the House of Commons* (2 vols., London, 1948-9). The collection of private acts authorizing the construction of railways is in the House of Lords Records at the Palace of Westminster.

24 Lieutenant-Colonel Sir Frederic Smith of the Royal Engineers was appointed at £900 a year. In 1842 Smith retired and was succeeded by Colonel Charles William Pasley (General Sir Charles Pasley). The railway board then consisted of the chief, who was also head of the statistical branch, the inspector-general at £570, the law and corresponding clerk at £500, the registrar at £260, one clerk and five messengers, one office keeper and one doorkeeper.

25 Ramsay, Sir James (1812-60), Marquis of Dalhousie; Harrow and Christ Church, Oxford; President of the Board of Trade, 1845; Governor-General of India, 1847-56. He is famous for his very able administration in India.

Industrial Design

GOVERNMENT SCHOOLS

THE design of an industrial product may be determined ultimately by the taste of the buyer, but it is also partly determined by the nature of the material of which it is made, the capacity of the artisan and his tools or machinery, and the purpose it is to serve. The æsthetic quality of an object has always been subject to these limitations and it has been considered in good taste if it is made of an appropriate material, well constructed, and designed to serve its function efficiently. Thus before the widespread use of machinery, household and other objects used by most people were of rudimentary construction and honest pattern. They were sturdily built of the cheapest available material according to simple, well-proven design. Decoration was often applied but it was chaste and followed a traditional style. Thus peasant furniture, household furnishings, and architecture were seldom ugly.

On the other hand, the rich, leisured, educated aristocracy were able to afford the use of exotic materials, expensive workmanship, and elaborate design and decoration, but their taste was prescribed by rigid canons which assumed the dependence of material and design on function and the effect of decoration. Thus they patronized the artist and craftsman, and the three together, in a kind of partnership, created products of beauty. Individual whims were tolerated because they were the results of eccentricity or humour rather than of ignorance. Both the eighteenth-century farmhouse and the large country house remain monuments to such conditions.

By 1830 something had gone wrong. Industrial design was hideous. Industrialism meant that the possibilities of the new machines seemed limitless. Out of many new materials, machinists could stamp, mould, or carve parts that, when fitted together, made up an object which looked as though it had been produced by a craftsman. A bedstead for a farmhouse formerly was a simple wooden frame, or if it was for a palace, it was luxurious but designed by an artist and carved by a master. However, with the new techniques of industrialism, with the easy fitting together of parts stamped out of metal by machines, parts imitative of hand-carving in wood, the bedstead blossomed and sprouted out into a full-blown exuberance more commensurate with the growing wealth of the public than with good sense.[1] The obvious and elaborate ornamentation delighted the *nouveaux riches*. But they did not have to be particularly rich to buy the new products, for manufacturers were able to lower their costs steadily and, realizing that their profits depended upon large sales, they charged less. Thus their shams and imitations were soon cheap enough for everybody. Then, too, people were getting more money with which to buy and to encourage the manufacturers. No longer limited by the quality or nature of materials, the skill of workmanship, or the function for which their products were designed, they produced a wonderful variety of cheap furniture, household furnishings, and other objects. With all limitations gone, the manufacturer concerned himself only with profits and catered to a public clamouring for more and more, cheaper and cheaper, products. Quantity conquered quality, the canons of taste were ignored, and the victory of vulgarity was complete. The classic country house of the eighteenth century gave way to the Great Exhibition of 1851.

The aristocratic patron retained his title, but he lost his leadership in matters of taste to the rising middle classes (and became middle class himself), the craftsman was replaced by the machinist, whose skill exceeded his understanding, and the artist was ignored. With taste dictated by an uneducated public, an ingenious machinist was better qualified to design industrial products than an artist. As a result of their rejection by society, artists went off and founded cults of their own and practised art for art's sake, or for the artists' sake. This conscious cultism completed the separation of art from manufacture, and ensured the rule of vulgarity.[2]

Inevitably there were the few critics who protested against the bad quality and design of manufactures. They admired the superior design of German and French products, and although techniques of manufacture were not so developed in those countries and machines had not as yet entirely replaced craftsmen, they suggested that when the foreigners had caught up with the British in mass production and could match them in cost, they would be able to outsell the British. The industrial designer or manufacturer, catering to a public with little discrimination, was bound to lose out in the race for bigger sales in those areas without such debased public taste. And one of the reasons for the continued superiority of foreign designs and public taste was the maintenance of government schools of design. Such schools had long been operated in France and Germany. Those at the Gobelin tapestry and Sèvres china works and the Lyons silk pattern schools were only the most famous. Endeavouring to make an artist of the industrial designer, they taught the techniques of better design, its history, and gave him some appreciation of the problems of good taste. From these schools foreign manufacturers hired men of training and experience. In England, where there were no such schools, an employer stamped out a product designed only by one of the workmen, a man who might have no qualifications. Even if manufacturers did realize that their designs were poor, they could not afford to maintain schools individually, and co-operation in such an effort was almost unheard of. Three attempts to establish schools had been made during the eighteenth century, but they had accomplished little. In 1727 the Board of Trustees for the Encouragement of Manufactures had been established in Scotland; in 1731, the Dublin Society; and in 1754, the Society of Arts in London.[3] They offered instruction in design, but their inadequate funds, the disinterest of the manufacturers, and their novelty, minimized their influence. The British Museum, organized in 1753, and the Royal Academy, in 1765, stimulated interest in the fine arts, and also probably had some effect upon industrial design. But in the eighteenth century, machine production had not yet debased design sufficiently to warrant such schools. By 1830 the machine's victory was devastating. The schools were required.

Another strong argument in favour of schools of design was offered by Henry Cole. He said :

The public, according to its ignorance or will, indicates its wants, the manufacturer supplies them, and the artisan only does what the manufacturer bids him. The improvement of manufactures is, therefore, altogether dependent upon the public sense of the necessity of it, and the public ability to judge between what is good and bad in Art. . . . In order to improve manufactures [we must] *elevate the Art education of the whole people*, and not merely to each artisans who are the servants of manufacturers, who themselves are the servants of the public.[4]

With a public educated to demand good design, the manufacturers would be forced to employ trained men who had been taught the principles of design. Thus they would soon realize the value of such schools and give them support, but the Government had to establish them in the first place and create the public demand for quality.

The great wars against Napoleon stimulated British industry as much as they stifled all political and social reform. The Government was too busy maintaining social order and reorganizing its finances to allow reform, and private enterprise was busy with all the problems of post-war re-adjustment. But with the twenties and the war receding into the past, men once again became conscious of all manner of things which had to be changed, even in the realm of the arts. The National Gallery was established for the encouragement of interest in the fine arts; something should be done for the improvement of the industrial arts. In 1827 the *Westminster Review* said that in pottery, cotton printing, paper staining, carpet weaving and in other industries :

The value or demand depends often as much, or more, on the art, or the design, and taste, than on the texture or fabric; and while that demand will depend on the taste of the consumers, so, as the arts improve, it will become more fastidious; as it has already done, in reality, to the exclusion of many of our own manufactures of taste from foreign markets. And the proof is incontrovertible, even from one fact alone; namely, the success which attended Mr. Wedgwood, to whom we really owe our entire commerce in the article of pottery; an example, if example could effect anything, of the value of art in commerce, or in money-making. And thus it is, that France has driven us from the market in numerous articles of manufacture and commerce, and chiefly in consequence of the superiority; while bidding fair, as its commercial influence and means shall increase, and as its fabrics attain a higher level, to supersede us in everything where taste or art is required. ... And it effects this by education. It possesses schools of art for workmen : the lowest are taught to draw, for without this it is vain to suppose that taste can be acquired; since taste is knowledge.[5]

The growing realization of the inferiority of British design was exemplified by the architectural chauvinism of the thirties. When Queen Victoria and Palmerston made Charles Barry abandon his Renaissance design for the new Houses of Parliament at Westminster and substitute English perpendicular, they only expressed a wide popular feeling. And Pugin, in conscientiously utilizing all the decorative arts to realize the new national style, exposed the deterioration of English design.[6] In disgust against the new machine imitation, he trained a whole corps of craftsmen to recover the skill of medieval builders. The climate of opinion which welcomed the new national style and allowed Pugin his extravagant return to the past had already prepared the way for a Parliamentary inquiry.

In 1835, William Ewart, the Liberal son of a Liverpool merchant, secured the selection of a large committee to " inquire into the best means of extending a knowledge of the Arts, and of the Principles of Design among the People (especially the Manufacturing Population) of the Country; [and] to inquire into the Constitution, Management, and Effects of Institutions connected with the Arts." [7]

The committee accomplished little the first year, and so continued its inquiry, publishing its report in August of 1836. It agreed with the many critics out-of-doors that there was a lamentable deficiency of taste and artistic knowledge in the design of manufactures, and that English commercial art was inferior to that of continental countries. It considered English design which followed the styles of Louis XIV or of the Tudors inferior and of spurious origin. It found that as a result the French and others were outselling the English in goods which depended for their appeal upon their design, goods like silk ribbons and shawls, and other luxury products. The main reason for the superiority of foreign design was that other countries operated schools of design. France as many as eighty, and Bavaria, thirty-three. Continental manufacturers were supplied amply with well-trained and experienced resident designers or artists, whereas the larger English manufacturers resorted to the necessarily occasional use of ill-trained itinerant designers, and the smaller, to just any workman in the factory, a man with no training at all. The Mechanics' Institutions taught mechanics, not design. The committee pointed out that :

> [To England], a peculiarly manufacturing nation, the connexion between art and manufactures is most important;—and for this merely economical reason (were there no higher motive), it equally imports us to encourage art in its loftier attributes; since it is admitted that the cultivation of the more exalted branches of design tends to advance the humblest pursuits of industry, while the connexion of art with manufacture has often developed the genius of the greatest masters in design.[8]

It recommended that local schools should be supported, museums should be extended and encouraged, that more attention should be paid to the exhibition of pictures so that better examples of taste would be more available to the public, and that the copyright laws should be changed so that designers would receive more adequate protection for their designs.

The Board of Trade did not wait for the report to be published. In July, it wrote a letter to the Treasury saying that the establishment of a school of design to be operated at Government expense had long been considered desirable, and had now been recommended by a strong committee, and therefore it asked that the Treasury add £1,500 to the estimates to allow the establishment of the school. The Treasury approved, and the Board appointed a committee to organize the school. The committee consisted of Thomson, the President of the Board of Trade, as chairman, of Bellenden Ker, the expert on legislative drafting, Sir William Copeland, a porcelain manufacturer, and the Lord Mayor of London, and four artists. At their first meeting in December 1836, they outlined the objects of the school, emphasizing that it should teach industrial design, not give training in fine arts. After a lengthy exchange of correspondence with the Commissioners of Woods and Forests, they were given the two rooms in Somerset House formerly occupied by the Royal Academy to use for the school. On the first of June the next year, 1837, the school opened.

During its first few years, the one school in London was considered an experiment and its size was kept small. But meanwhile, in 1838, the well-known painter William Dyce was appointed director, and while trying to build up the school, travelled abroad and made a thorough investigation of foreign schools. His intelligent report, published in 1840, reaffirmed the opinion of the parliamentary committee of the need of local schools. The government was persuaded to authorize the grant of £10,000 for the formation of provincial schools at Birmingham, Glasgow, Manchester, and York.

A council of about twenty prominent artists and men interested in industrial design had been appointed to superintend the management of the schools. Dyce reported to them in 1840 that students received elementary training in the drawing of ornament and of the human figure, the drawing from plaster, and in modelling and colouring. They received instruction in design applicable to special branches of industry such as fabrics, which " admit only of the application of design under certain conditions." They also studied the history of taste in manufactures, the various styles of ornament and " such theoretical knowledge as [was] calculated to improve the tastes of the pupils, and to add to their general acquaintance with art." [9] The emphasis was entirely on the training in industrial design, not in the fine arts.

The management of the schools received steady criticism. They could not please everyone. The director, who managed the schools, was immediately responsible to a council, appointed by the Board of Trade. Its task was to make sure that the schools taught industrial design and not fine arts or mechanical engineeering. The Council was continually asked to support schools established for other purposes. For example, in answer to a letter from the Liverpool Mechanics Institution requesting funds, the Council of Design wrote that since its schools were still considered to be an experiment, it could support only a few of them, and to insure the success of the schools, they had to be carefully watched. Other schools like the Mechanics Institution should be managed by a local committee. The administration of the schools of design must not become too closely associated with that of schools run for different purposes, or the Council would not be able to retain the close relationship between the local schools and the Council then established.[10] Wearied of the many problems of management, Dyce left the schools of design in 1843 and returned to his painting. He was followed as superintendent by Charles Heath Wilson.

Criticism continued to plague the Council. Manufacturers complained that students were not properly trained and that they lacked technical knowledge, and therefore tended to drift into fine art instead of finding employment in industrial art. The result was the appointment of a special committee of the Council in 1846 to examine the management, with the secretary of the Board of Trade, J. G. Shaw-Lefevre, as chairman.[11] The committee severely criticized the schools for not fulfilling their function. Their teaching of industrial design was vitiated by their tendency to imitate the fine arts rather than to study the technique of ornamental design. In response, *The Times*, recognizing that the Government had to train a whole generation in design before real progress could be made, considered the schools a success.[12] The next year another committee was appointed with Richard Monckton Milnes in the chair. Both committees agreed that there should be more careful supervision of the teaching. As a result the Board of Trade appointed a committee of instruction consisting of five men to supervise instruction, to exercise all powers of the Council, and to control all the affairs of the school. Despite the efforts towards centralization and the increased efficiency, the new arrangement was still not effective. In April of 1848 the Board of Trade again took up the problem.

> My Lords resumed the consideration of the arrangements for managing the School of Design. The experience of the last four months has shown that the business can be conducted with facility by the officers of the Board of Trade aided by the advice of Sir R. Westmacott, W. Richmond, and W. Poynter. [The artists.] My lords think, moreover, that the great importance of the several institutions; and the amount of the pecuniary aid given to them by Government require that the head of the Board of Trade should be made more directly responsible for their management than at present. My Lords therefore deem it right that in future the minutes of the Committee should receive the confirmation of the President or Vice-President before they are acted on, and that the President or Vice-President shall, if they think fit, preside at the meetings of the Committee.

This arrangement will render it unnecessary that any functions should henceforth be performed by the original council, and my Lords are therefore pleased to dissolve that body, and to constitute the following persons as the Committee of Management of the School. Sir Richard Westmacott, George Richmond, Ambrose Poynter, J. G. Shaw Lefevre, Stafford Northcote and the joint secretaries.[13]

Later that year the President of the Board of Trade reported to the Committee on Miscellaneous Expenditure that the schools were now managed successfully and therefore no change was recommended. However, he was deluded, for in 1849 a select committee of the House of Commons with Milner Gibson as chairman reported that the Board of Trade should exercise still closer control, should appoint all masters and appoint paid inspectors to visit the schools.[14] There were sixteen provincial schools with about 3,000 pupils under instruction. As a result, the Board now directed that Herbert, Redgrave, and Townsend, as joint headmasters of the School at Somerset House, " should undertake the entire conduct of the school, with direct responsibility to the Board." Everyone agreed that the purpose of the schools was good, but that their management was faulty and that their achievement was disappointing.[15]

In the spring of 1851 an exhibition of the work of students of the schools of design was held at Marlborough House, but public attention was focused farther west on the great iron and glass structure nearing completion in Hyde Park. The Great Exhibition, 1851, was about to open. The story of its history is well known; how Henry Cole and Prince Albert, together with Joseph Paxton, built the wonderful great greenhouse, one of the first examples of modern architecture, and brought together the biggest collection of manufactures ever. The displays were imaginative, ingenious and skilfully contrived.[16] The exhibition remains the great monument to the vulgarity of the early industrialism. The exhibits have long since been ridiculed sufficiently, but their grossness suggests one reason why the schools of design never really achieved the success which some had hoped for. How could they prosper in such a milieu? One of the headmasters of the London School of Design thus analysed the cause of their failure :

The English public, and the English manufacturers as a body, are hardly yet awake on the question of design. Government has established schools of ornamental art in many of our large manufacturing towns for the purpose of spreading genuine taste, and educating our workmen; but they are as yet a forced product, and have hardly anywhere, after ten years of struggle, won the warm support of the local manufacturer. Even in this Great Exhibition the question of design was nearly overlooked, and the work of the designer left without a place. His name was not necessarily coupled with the fabrics or manufactures his skill had designed or decorated, and his reward therefore was left to the good feeling of his employer.[17]

In response to continued criticism, the Board of Trade once again reorganized the administration of the schools of design. A Department of Practical Art was established in 1852; Henry Cole accepted the position of General Superintendent. In August 1853, the schools were moved from Somerset House to Marlborough House. But early in the next year this department was enlarged to include all local institutions for the advancement of practical science : the Government School of Mines and Science applied to the Arts, the Museum of Practical Geology, the Geological Survey, the Museum of Irish Industry, the Royal Dublin Society. The new department was now called the Department of Science and Art.[18] Henry Cole was to be the secretary for art and Lyon Playfair the secretary for science. The inquiry into the means of carrying out this reorganization had been headed by J. Emerson Tennent, and it was the determination of Prince Albert that had pushed it through.[19] In 1854 the London Seamen's School and the Nautical School were transferred to the Department.

To complement the teaching in the schools, exhibits were organized from time to time to present good design to students and to the public. In 1852, with the close co-operation of the Board of Trade, a permanent display was organized. The best examples of woven fabric, metalwork, enamels, ceramics and wood carvings were purchased from the Great Exhibition and exhibited at Marlborough House where the Queen had given forty rooms to the Department. Among the displays some were included to show bad design.[20] Those manufacturers so honoured complained effectively. Meanwhile, through the efforts of Prince Albert, part of the proceeds of £186,000 from the Great Exhibition was spent in the purchase of land and the preparation of buildings at South Kensington for a Museum of Manufactures. In 1857 the schools of design and the exhibition of manufactures were moved there, and that same year, their management was transferred from the Board of Trade to the Privy Council. From this date, despite the efforts of Henry Cole, the emphasis of the training was to shift from industrial design to fine arts. In effect the original purpose of the schools of design had not been realized, despite the constant effort of the Board of Trade. Only one hundred years later with the establishment of the Council of Industrial Design would British manufacturers recognize the value of such schools.[21]

REGISTRY OF DESIGNS AND INTERNATIONAL COPYRIGHT

Inventions had long been safeguarded in the letters patent or charters granted by the Privy Council to the inventor or manufacturer. The Board of Trade customarily advised the Council. However, in the eighteen-thirties, the Board became exclusively responsible for the protection of the design of ornamental patterns. These designs were offered a copyright by the Designs Registry Office set up by the Board of Trade in 1839.

Previous to the act which led to the establishment of that office, three acts, passed in 1787, 1789, and 1799, had offered a few months' protection to patterns printed on linen, cotton, calico, and muslin.[22] In the following years, manufacturers began printing woollens, silks, and mixtures not covered by these acts. They naturally clamoured for protection for the new materials as well as protection for a longer period of time for those materials already covered. At a meeting in 1831 they drew up a request that the Board of Trade appoint a board of commissioners to register designs and safeguard their protection, and during the next few years they continued to petition for the establishment of the registry office.

By 1838, the Board of Trade was convinced that a new act was advisable, and the President, Thomson, asked Mr. Unthank to draft a bill to be presented in the next session. It provided for the registration of all designs and their protection for twelve months; but since the calico printers objected to compulsory registration, the bill was amended so that it did not apply to them. Two acts were passed. The first extended the copyright to wool, silk, hair, or mixed fabrics. The second, called the Designs Copyright Act, or the Registration Act, gave a copyright to metal articles for three years, to others for one year, and to designs for all articles of manufacture except lace and those provided for in previous legislation.[23] In June 1839, the Registry Office was set up " at the lowest possible level." Francis B. Long, the registrar, was to be assisted by a chief clerk, a junior clerk, and a messenger or porter.[24]

A select committee in 1840 examined the whole problem of the registration for copyright, and during the forties, various acts were passed modifying or extending the rules. The barrister, Emerson Tennent, was the indefatigable supporter of the bills.[25] And although the details in the rules were changed from time to time, the registry office was a success and its business continually increased. By 1853 its personnel had increased to nine men : the registrar, his assistant, three clerks, an office keeper, two messengers, and a printer. The Board of Trade solved this particular responsibility with a minimum of effort.

Another similar problem which concerned the President of the Board of Trade was an international copyright to protect authors from piracy of their works. Authors were bitter about the loss of rights for publications in foreign countries, and Thomson became particularly interested during the thirties in reaching agreements with other countries which would give authors the same protection there as they received in England. It was to him " one important feature of that larger intercourse between nations which was his cherished ideal." [26] A bill had been introduced to allow the government to treat with other countries for a copyright, but had been defeated. Harriet Martineau said that its defeat was due to a stupid speech by Macaulay.[27] But Thomson persevered and secured passage for a bill in 1838 which authorized the Government to enter into treaty arrangements for international protection.[28] Thereafter appropriate negotiations were carried on mainly by the Foreign Office, but with the encouragement of the Board of Trade. Amending acts were passed to please Prussia and other countries, and it was only after years of effort on the part of the President of the Board of Trade, the Foreign Secretary, and the Prime Minister, that effective agreements were reached.[29]

The schools of design did not long remain with the Board, and the office for the registration of designs was a minor duty. International copyright was not a concern of the Board itself, only of its chief officers. Yet the Government's relationship to these three activities was largely defined by the Board and its personnel. The regulation of the great merchant shipping industry became the primary responsibility of the Board and largely determined its transformation, but the schools of industrial design, the office for the registration of designs and the treaties for international copyright remain part of this history.

NOTES

[1] There was one good result of the new beds. Bugs liked to live in wooden bedsteads. Thus the use of metal ones " was a marked hygienic advance." Workmen got two hours more sleep a night, which was equal in a week to a day's holiday. G. W. Robertson Scott, *The Day Before Yesterday* (London, 1951), p. 73.

[2] For a brief account of the withdrawal of the artist " from such squalor " see Nikolaus Pevsner, *Pioneers of Modern Design* (New York, 1949), p. 8. The artist was rejected as servant or friend and became a self-appointed priest, a misunderstood genius.

[3] The origin of the Board was an article in the Treaty of Union which set aside a large sum of money due from England for the promotion of fisheries and manufactures of Scotland. The Dublin Society was granted £500 by the Board of Trade as late as 1849. See John C. L. Sparkes, *Schools of Art* (London, 1884), p. 21.

[4] Frank P. Brown, *South Kensington and its Art Training* (London, 1912), p. 13.

[5] *Westminster Review*, VII (April 1827), p. 284.

[6] See Kenneth Clark, *The Gothic Revival* (London, 1950).

[7] *P. P.*, 1835, V.

[8] *P. P.*, 1836, IX. The Mechanics' Institutions, established after 1824 by George Birkbeck and others, did not have enough funds to teach industrial design as well as mechanics. The Edinburgh School of Art for Mechanics, founded in 1822 by Leonard Horner, younger brother of the Factory Inspector (Francis), also suffered from lack of funds.

[9] BT 1, 362.

[10] BT 1, 404.

[11] Shaw-Lefevre, Sir John George (1797-1879), Eton and Trinity College, Cambridge; barrister, 1825; under-secretary to E. S. Stanley (later Lord Derby) at Colonial Office, 1833; on commission which founded colony of Australia, 1834; commissioner for carrying into effect new Poor Law Amendment Act, 1834; Joint-Assistant Secretary to Board of Trade, 1841-8; on Ecclesiastical Commission, 1847; deputy-clerk of the Parliaments, 1848, and clerk, 1855-75; and held other offices.

[12] *The Times* (London), December 27th, 1847, p. 4.

[13] BT 5, 57.

[14] *P. P.*, 1849, VIII.

[15] The *Journal of Design and Manufactures*, Vol. I, 1849, said that the council did not work well during the forties because not one of the artists was an ornamentalist, and the manufacturers seldom attended. In 1844 the council was increased from twenty to twenty-five men, but it still did not work well; and in 1847, when the Board of Trade took over more directly, the management continued to be weak. Poynter, one of the chief members, was incompetent. And the members of the Board were already too busy. The *Journal* said this about Lefevre, who was chiefly responsible at the Board: his " good-natured tact causes him to be made a sort of omnibus commissioner— Commissioner for managing Church Revenues in two capacities, Commissioner for investigating the British Museum, Commissioner for settling the Scotch Annuity Tax, in short, Commissioner for everything which needs to be coaxed into quietude—in addition to being Clerk of the Parliament. If he has any leisure, he must want it for sleep, and cannot afford to give it to the School of Design." Pp. 24-6.

[16] Many realized the value of the Exhibition for promoting sales abroad of English goods. H.M. Stationery Office as well as private publishers printed illustrated catalogues which were widely distributed abroad.

[17] John C. L. Sparkes, *Schools of Art*, p. 61.

[18] The School of Mines had been established in 1851. The practical nature of all these institutions was constantly emphasized. The Museum of Practical Geology was also established in 1851, at the insistence of Sir Henry de la Beche.

[19] The estimated annual cost of the various activities follows:

	£
Government School of Mines and of Science applied to the Arts	800
Museum of Practical Geology	5,272
Geological Survey	5,500
Museum of Irish Industry	3,348
The Royal Dublin Society	6,340
The Department of Practical Art and the Schools of Design	17,900

See Margaret Reeks, *Register of the Associates and Old Students of the Royal School of Mines and History of the Royal School of Mines* (London, 1920), p. 67. The Civil Service estimate for the Department had risen to £80,000 in 1855. *P. P.*, 1855, 31.

[20] Dickens describes this, in Mr. Crump's words: " I could have cried, Sir. I was ashamed of the pattern of my own trousers, for I saw a piece of them hung up there as a horror. I dared not pull out my pocket-handkerchief while anyone was by, lest I should be seen dabbling the perspiration from my forehead with a wreath of coral. I saw it all; when I went home I found that I had been living among horrors up to that hour. The paper in my parlour contains four birds of paradise, besides bridges and pagodas." As quoted by Nikolaus Pevsner, *High Victorian Design* (London, 1951), p. 152.

[21] Opinions change. John Sparkes, writing in 1884, said: " The evidence afforded by the International Exhibition of 1862 as to the marked improvement observable in our art-manufactures since the first great display in Hyde Park in 1851, was abundant and decisive; and it would be unreasonable to deny that this improvement, and, indeed, the general advance of artistic taste in this country, may be attributed in great measure to the influences, direct and indirect, of the Schools of Art." *Schools of Art*, p. 74. Nikolaus

Pevsner, writing in 1951, says: "Yet with all their zest and ingenuity Cole and his friends achieved nothing. The standards at the 1862 Exhibition were just as confused and the taste just as inflated [as in 1851]." *High Victorian Design*, pp. 152-3. Mr. C. H. Gibbs-Smith, of the Victoria and Albert Museum, who has studied this period extensively, regards Henry Cole as one of the few really good Civil Servants of the century. It may also be said that the opinion of Prince Albert has been improving. Certainly these two men deserve unreserved credit for their attempt to improve industrial design.

22 27 Geo. III c. 38; 29 Geo. III c. 19; and 39 Geo. III c. 23.

23 2 & 3 Vict. c. 13; and 2 & 3 Vict. c. 17.

24 BT 5, 46. The Board recommended that the salaries of the personnel be £400 for the registrar, £250 for the chief clerk, £90 for the junior clerk, and £60 for the messenger. The Treasury was expected to pay the salaries until the fees for registration were sufficient. The Board considered that this office was very much in the nature of an experiment. One of the reasons that the bill passed readily was that the maintenance of the office would cost the Government little or nothing.

25 *P. P.*, 1849, VI. In 1843 the calico printers gave Tennent a complete silver service. *The Times* (London), January 3rd, 1843, p. 3.

26 Adam Shortt, *Lord Sydenham* (New York, 1926), p. 51.

27 H. Martineau, *Autobiography*, I, 261. The speech is unrecorded in *Parl. Deb.*

28 1 & 2 Vict. c. 59.

29 Only with the Berne Convention of 1887 were substantial agreements among many countries reached. The U.S.A. passed its first bill offering some protection to foreigners in 1891.

III

Merchant Shipping

Introduction

THE British merchant marine was the biggest in the world. It was also the worst. Its ships were unseaworthy; its officers and seamen irresponsible; and its owners negligent. Each year during the thirties two thousand persons were drowned and over five hundred ships worth over £3,000,000 were lost. Only a merchant navy so large could sustain such losses. During the French wars they could be attributed to the exigencies of war, but after 1815 peace made such excuses untenable. The appalling losses could only be explained by the negligence of the owners, builders, masters and seamen.

Harriet Martineau, returning from the United States, described in her autobiography the bad condition of her ship.

> Our cargo is partly turpentine, the vessel leaks, and so do the turpentine casks; and what comes up by the pumps is so nauseous as to cause much complaint among the passengers. There was no time at New York to get the copper bottom mended; and the crew are hard worked with the pumping. The captain says if the leak increases, he shall employ the steerage passengers at the pumps.[1]

In the forties, British consuls, stationed in many foreign ports and therefore in a good position to compare the British marine with that of other countries, were asked to report their opinion. Nearly all described the inferiority of the British ships and crews.

> The sole object with British shipowners in the Baltic trade appears to be, to officer and man their ships at the cheapest rate. The only qualifications they deem necessary in a shipmaster are, that insurance can be obtained upon a vessel placed under his command—and the lowest possible rate of remuneration for his services.

I am sorry to state that . . . the British Commercial Marine is, at present, in a worse condition than that of any other nation.

With regret I say it, there are not, taken as a whole, a more troublesome, thoughtless set of men, to use the mildest term, to be met with, than British seamen. Only lately a master left his vessel, which was loaded with a valuable cargo and ready for sea, and was, after several days' search, found in a brothel; his mate was very little better than himself, and his people, following his example, a set of drunkards.[2]

All consuls substantiated what many others knew to be true : British ships were inferior and the shipmasters and crews were demoralized.

Before the modification of the navigation acts in the twenties, British ships had monopolized the trade between ports within the empire and enjoyed many advantages trading between a port in the empire and a foreign port. Furthermore, the navy had virtually swept all French and continental shipping off the seas during the wars and had successfully cut out American competition on many routes. British shipowners, with no competition, became lethargic and set in their ways. Meanwhile the Americans began to encroach on the trade in both the Spanish and British empires. Building fast ships so that they could outrun Spanish and British patrol boats and offering better service than their older competitors, they stole more and more of the trade. At the same time British manufacturers and merchants, underselling all others on the world market, succeeded in their campaign for freer trade and forced Parliament to modify the navigation acts in favour of freer competition. American and colonial ships were then able to compete with British ships, even within the empire. British shipowners strongly objected but were outvoted by the other groups who wanted cheap transport for their goods so that they could sell more abroad. American and colonial ships after all could serve the manufacturers as well as British. In 1815 the American marine was only one-half the size of the British; by 1835, it was two thirds as large. The American continued to increase faster and with the discovery of gold in California in 1849 and in Australia in 1851 and the consequent demand for fast ships of the type of the American clipper, the American marine soon overtook the British.[3]

The Americans and British North Americans competed success-fully because they took advantage of British lethargy. While the latter tended to stick to established habits, the innovators quickly accepted any device which would give them the advantage. In the transatlantic timber trade, for example, they used old cheap ships, whereas in the mail and passenger service they used first-class fast ships, and as early as 1816 they scheduled sailings. But in addition to the vigour of youth they had other advantages. Their ships cost less to build. While the British had to import timber, they had a plentiful and cheap supply at home. Their labour cost less than British. And naturally their maintenance costs were much lower than the British, for it took a good deal of timber and constant replacement to keep ships afloat in those days. Moreover, they paid their seamen only half the wages of the British and were not compelled to carry as many men aboard. Whereas by law the British had to carry four seamen and one apprentice for each 100 tons, the Americans and others were free to carry as few as they liked.[4]

These advantages were only aggravated by the general glut of shipping. Although during the earlier years of this period the number of ships did not increase, the amount of available shipping did. Ships were being built larger and sailed faster so that one ship made more trips during the year and carried more. Further-more, with improved navigation and the use of steam tugs to tow sailing ships in and out of port, ships more frequently sailed in winter instead of laying over. Thus the same tonnage of shipping carried increasingly greater tonnage of freight. No longer pro-tected from foreign competition, outbid by Americans and others on many routes where they formerly were secure, and suffering from an oversupply of tonnage, British shipowners remained in a depressed state throughout the thirties and forties.

Discouraged and apprehensive of bankruptcy, they responded to the growing competition by cutting costs and saving rather than by investing capital in improvements and innovations in ships or in navigation. They spent too little on the construction of a ship, on its maintenance, and on the training and welfare of the crew. The result was a general deterioration in the comparative quality of British shipping. Just about everything was wrong.[5] Ships were badly and cheaply constructed. *Lloyd's Register* encouraged negligent building because it automatically classified all new ships as first-class for a few years, then at the same age for all ships it gave them an inferior classification. Thus it mattered little what kind of wood was used in their construction and how well they were maintained. Repair in general was much neglected because rotted or broken timbers could often be hidden and certain beams and planking would receive full stress only in a storm which the ship might never encounter. Furthermore, design was faulty. Flat bottoms were frequently used so that ships could rest on the bottom of harbours at low tide. And the method of tonnage measurement, upon which port and light dues were based, encouraged owners to build ships which were too long for their width. A constant complaint was that ships carried inadequate equipment of all kinds for investigation, for repair, and for life-saving. Ships were improperly or excessively loaded, especially those in the Atlantic timber trade where the bulky cargo was loaded on deck with the result that in a slight storm the ships became unseaworthy.

Masters and mates were unqualified; they received little or no schooling, had too little experience and were not examined for competence or knowledge, even of navigation. They were frequently drunken and irresponsible. Seamen were even more the subject of complaint. Ill-fed, badly quartered, irregularly paid, they were often cheated into signing-on by crimps, and so abused on board that they deserted in the first port of call.

Navigational aids, although improved every year, were still inadequate. Lighthouses were too few and too weak. Light and pilot dues were sometimes too high. Charts were inaccurate and there were not enough harbours of refuge.

The method of insurance did not encourage the bad owners to reform, for although they paid higher rates than the good owners who were known to be better risks, they were usually paid in full for their losses. Underwriters were silent in the agitation for improvement because they received high enough fees to cover their losses; losses which were small since so many were responsible for the loss of any one ship that no one underwriter felt a single loss unduly. The method of insuring ships continued to be blamed for losses for many years. As late as the seventies, Samuel Plimsoll blamed ship losses on the indifference of the underwriters.

And finally there was the uncertain role of the government, for although laissez faire in business was the goal, shipping was too much involved with the military well-being of the empire to be left entirely alone. For a long time there had been various regulations concerned with shipping; many were part of the old code of the navigation acts. The confusion among the acts themselves was considerable but the confusion among the departments of the Government as to which was responsible for their administration was even worse. The Admiralty was responsible for the supply of seamen, the Treasury for the customs, the Colonial Office and the Land and Emigration Commissioners for passengers. In all, nine departments were involved in the shipping regulations. The amount of semi-official correspondence necessary for a decision was frequently enough to delay it until it was no longer of use. It was too easy for the person responsible in any department to refer the question to another department and thus avoid responsibility. Yet if he were succeeded by someone with a different view, the department might take vigorous action to enforce an act. In the confused administration of the shipping business, the only consistent policy on the part of the Government seemed to be the withdrawal of all protection for British shipping, and this was the one interpretation of laissez faire which the owners feared. Indeed the shipping interest was in a state of unrest.

Then, as now, the recognized way to interest public opinion in any cause or to put pressure on the Government was to hold public meetings, organize a society with distinguished and aristocratic patrons, then to publish pamphlets and articles, and finally to petition Parliament and to introduce the appropriate bill. For many causes, a bill was not appropriate, but for almost every part of the complex shipping industry, an act was desired, at least by a few persons. The newspapers and journals had frequent accounts of public meetings called or organized by the few interested in a particular cause. If the meeting was successful and enough enthusiasm and funds were raised, usually a society or committee was organized to set up an office, to publicize and to organize other meetings. But often the funds were inadequate and the society was not formed. The individual or the few persons originally concerned with the reform carried on as best they could. Since several hundred thousand persons were employed in the large business of shipping, and many others followed particular phases of it, there were many organizations and groups advocating all kinds of reform. The shipping interest formed many local societies, and particular branches of it formed additional societies, such as the Liverpool Steamship Owners' Society. But most powerful was the General Shipowners' Society, organized in London in 1831 and formed to help the shipping interest throughout the country. It became more important than the provincial societies because it drew its main support from the largest and wealthiest port and operated in the national capital. At its first meeting one of its organizers suggested its function. " In every question connected with the shipping interest, it must be advisable that Government should have a body to whose sense and opinions at large they might refer." [6] Although it soon became the leading lobby for the shipping interest, it was only one of many. It was mainly concerned throughout the thirties and forties with the maintenance of protection but it also actively advanced many other causes. The shipowners ultimately failed on the issue of protection but their success in stalling or modifying or obtaining legislation in other areas cannot be overestimated.

There were many other groups or individuals concerned with shipping. Some were primarily devoted to the welfare of masters or mates, seamen or passengers, especially after 1834 when a good deal of the humanitarian sentiment in the cause of anti-slavery was translated to shipping. Others realized that the extravagant losses of cargoes and ships could be reduced by legislation or by governmental supervision. Still others had a special interest. They sought governmental support for the study of meteorology, they wanted a new method of tonnage measurement, or to improve the lot of the coalwhippers. In some cases the shipping interest opposed reform, especially if it meant more government. At other times the interest was quite divided or was in favour of some particular measure. Furthermore, the shipowners often changed their opinions.

With the interplay of interests and passions, there was a growing awareness of the bad state of shipping and of the need for Government action. Publicity, after all, was the chief weapon of all factions in their battle for reform. The shipowners advertised the bad economic state of British shipping in order to maintain Governmental protection and stave off regulation, whereas humanitarians and others advertised the bad treatment of emigrants so that the Government would have to inspect emigrant ships. Such organizations as the Royal Humane Society and the Royal National Institution for the Preservation of Life from Shipwreck, organized in 1824 to save shipwrecked mariners and to prevent shipwreck, stimulated interest in the problem.[7] *The Nautical Magazine*, started in 1832 and primarily devoted to hydrography, also published articles on many subjects such as proper stowage, tonnage and navigation, and included lists of wrecks and detailed accounts of how they happened. And in 1833 the two rival shipping registers, both of which were suffering from too few subscribers, voted to combine, and beginning in 1834, the new register, named after Lloyd of the original underwriters' house, became the handbook of all underwriters and general source of information on the condition of ships. It, too, offered information on the number and causes of wrecks. Within a few years *Lloyd's Register* employed as many as sixty-three surveyors and attained a circulation of over one thousand subscribers.

Pamphlets added to the agitation. For example, in 1830 Christopher Biden published his *Naval Discipline* in which he contrasted subordination with insubordination by a history of disasters at sea resulting from the latter, and emphasized the need for an Act of Parliament to establish better discipline. Another topical pamphlet was written in 1833 by a surveyor of shipbuilding and entitled *The True Causes of the Numerous Wrecks of Merchant Shipping and an Appeal to the Nation in the Causes of Humanity, to Apply the Remedy*.

By 1836 the pressure on Parliament was sufficient to force the House of Commons to select a committee " to inquire into the Causes of the Increased Number of Shipwrecks, with a view to ascertain whether such improvements might not be made in the Construction, Equipment and Navigation of Merchant Vessels, as would greatly diminish the annual Loss of Life and Property at Sea." [8] Whereas the inquiry of 1819 inquired into the losses of steamships only, and others had investigated various phases of shipping, this committee was to examine the whole industry. It first ascertained the amount of the losses and then determined the causes. It listed the latter under ten general headings : the defective construction of ships, the inadequacy of equipment, the imperfect state of repair, improper or excessive loading, inappropriateness of design, incompetence of masters and mates, drunkenness of officers and men, the operation of marine insurance, the want of harbours of refuge, and the imperfection of charts. In short, just about everything was wrong, and consequently the committee's report was uncompromising. It recommended the establishment of a marine board in London with powers to draw up a complete maritime code, to supervise the classification, building, and equipping of ships, to examine officers and to establish a registry office for seamen, to organize nautical schools for the younger apprentices, to conduct courts of inquiry for all shipwrecks and to settle disputes among officers, seamen and owners. The committee included in its demand to the legislature for action the statement :

> That it is a matter of the first importance to authorize, by enactment, the formation in London of a Mercantile Marine Board, to direct, superintend, and regulate the affairs of the Mercantile Marine of the United Kingdom, on such a plan of organization and control as shall unite a due regard to the private interests of the shipowners, merchants and underwriters, whose individual property may be embarked therein, with an equal attention to the public interests in the preservation of the national capital from destruction at sea; and, above all, in securing as far as possible the safety of the lives of those who may be engaged in navigating the ships and conducting the maritime commerce of the country.[9]

The Government of the day showed little interest in the report and left the drawing up of a bill incorporating the recommendations of the committee to a private member. James Silk Buckingham, a former journalist in India, long a critic of the Government and radical in politics, had for several years protested against the impressment and the exploitation of seamen. Knowing that the Government would do nothing about the report, he introduced a bill early the next year, 1837, providing for the establishment of a marine board which would have some of the duties outlined in the report.

Although its provisions were less thorough than those called for in the report, it immediately aroused a storm of protest. The issue was clear. Should a department or branch of the Government have executive power to regulate or interefere in the private industry of shipping? Joseph Hume debated during the introduction of the bill that, despite the danger of legislative interference in commercial matters, in this case it was demanded by circumstances. But opposed to Buckingham, Hume and the few others in favour of the bill, stood the majority of the House led by the Government. Thomson, the President of the Board of Trade, argued that the bill covered details not susceptible to legislation, and furthermore, one of the reasons for the greatness of the British merchant marine, was the lack of Governmental interference. France, he went on, had an admirable code of legislation but the problem was quite different because her marine was so much smaller (it was one sixth the size). He concluded with the statement that it was free competition which promoted progress. However, leave was granted to bring in the bill and it was read the first time.[10]

The shipping interest was strongly opposed. The General Shipowners' Society at its annual meeting in March had said that :

> Valuable as are some of the suggestions contained in this Report, they are satisfied, from practical experience, that many of the evils adverted to are not susceptible of remedy by Legislative enactments, and they anticipate the universal concurrence of Ship-Owners in their conviction, that compulsory regulations with respect to the form of construction and general mode of equipment of Ships, would be fraught with consequences so pernicious in themselves, and so subversive of the best interests of British Maritime Commerce, that it would be their duty strenuously to resist any such attempt.[11]

When the bill was introduced for a second reading in June, Thomson was even more outspoken in his opposition to it than he had been before. He said that it was impractical and so faulty in details that it would be impossible to carry it into law. Furthermore, the marine board would cost too much and it would have power beyond that of the legislature, in fact, it would have supreme power. The Vice-President of the Board of Trade, Henry Labouchere, said that the bill represented a vexatious interference with the shipping interest and would constitute a great blow to shipping.[12] And George F. Young, the President of the General Shipowners' Society, concluded his vigorous condemnation by calling the bill a "legislative monstrosity." The vote against a second reading was 176 to 28, with about half the members of the select committee voting against it.[13]

While any inclusive legislation was out of the question during the thirties, the government was involved every year in reforming various aspects of shipping. One year it was lighthouses, deck-cargoes, and a navigation school; the next, tonnage measurement, the supply of seamen, and pilotage. If the bill covered only one subject, it alienated fewer Members than if it were more thorough, and stood a better chance of being passed. Furthermore, these bills were pushed vigorously by a Member or an interest dedicated to a single cause. And because of their limited nature their need was more readily comprehended. George Young, for example, who so resolutely opposed any comprehensive bill, was in favour of a bill in 1839 to prohibit the carrying of timber on deck. During the inquiry before the bill he said :

> The interference of the Legislature with the transaction of commercial affairs I hold in principle to be exceedingly objectionable; but I think that when the interests of humanity are concerned, that general principle ought to give way; and that even if the shipowner were to sustain pecuniary loss therefrom, which in this instance I do not think he would, yet still the Legislature is not only justified in exercising such interference, but is bound to carry it into effect. I find precedents for such interference in the case of coaches, which are not permitted to carry luggage beyond a given height, lest the top weight upon them should overturn the coach, and endanger the lives of the passengers; I find the same interference in the Building Act, by which the construction of houses is subjected to the supervision of responsible officers; and I find, that in the conveyance of passengers in ships, the Legislature has, by the Passengers' Act, expressly interfered to determine the quantity of cargo, the state of the ship, as to sufficiency for the voyage, and the quantity and quality of the provisions supplied; I think therefore, that equally on principle, and under the authority

of precedent, the Legislature is both justified in interfering and is bound to interfere.[14]

This bill was passed, as were many others dealing with specific issues. Thus, bit by bit, a maritime code was under construction.

Meanwhile another suggestion of comprehensive legislation came in the report of the parliamentary committee selected in 1843 to inquire into the causes of shipwrecks.[15] The committee was a particularly strong one, including the leading representatives of the shipping interests together with the member of the Government most interested in the inquiry, W. E. Gladstone, the Vice-President of the Board of Trade. Although this committee agreed substantially with that of 1836 as to the causes of shipwreck, it confined its recommendations to specific details. It implied that in the future a central board should be set up, but it was not the appropriate time. The opposition of the shipowners to Parliamentary action remained strong. The committee of the General Shipowners' Society said that :

> Repeated experience has compelled your Committee to regard with no inconsiderable distrust the practical proceedings of Committees of the House of Commons. Whatever the motives and intentions of those at whose instigation they may be appointed, they afford so convenient a means for placing on record any description of opinion however remotely bearing on the subject of inquiry and the opinions thus recorded, however visionary, are so frequently rendered the basis of attempts at practical legislation ... [that we are suspicious of the present inquiry into the causes of shipwrecks].[16]

The wealthier and larger shipowners were able to maintain good ships and to discriminate in favour of capable officers and seamen. They understood the advantage of a good reputation, and operated on sufficient scale to be able to afford improvements. Furthermore, they realized that to anticipate public opinion in the matter of reform was to avoid Parliamentary interference. But the many marginal operators either could not afford the best in equipment or crews, or were indifferent, and it was mostly they who aroused the concern of a growing number of people. Articles and pamphlets continued to spread the conviction that the merchant marine was in a poor state. One of the most persistent reformers was James Murray of the Foreign Office. Aware of the consular reports which referred to the inferiority of British ships and crews, he became convinced that nothing short of a marine board responsible for the administration of the shipping code was adequate. In the process of collecting evidence, he sent a circular in 1843 to all consuls asking their opinion of the British merchant marine as compared to those of foreign countries. In it, he stated his purpose :

> I am particularly desirous of gaining information in regard to instances which have come under your observation of the incompetency of British shipmasters to manage their vessels and their crews, whether arising from deficiency of knowledge of practical navigation and seamanship, or of moral character, particularly want of sobriety. . . . My object is to show the necessity for more authoritative steps on the part of Her Majesty's Government to remedy what appears to be an evil, detrimental to, and seriously affecting the character of, our commercial marine, and therefore advantageous to foreign rivals, whose merchant vessels are said to be exceedingly well-manned and navigated.[17]

Of the seventy-five reports sent back in answer to Murray's request, seventy-two stated that British shipping was declining compared to foreign shipping. Their reasons for the decline repeated many of those found by the select committee, but also many cited the confusion resulting from the various acts and their administration as a contributing cause. Many recommended the establishment of a department of commercial marine. Murray concluded his circular letter to other departments of the Government with the statement that the mercantile community looked to the Board of Trade in regard to everything relating to trade, and that that Board should set up a special department of commercial marine, particularly to deal with other departments of the Government concerned with the industry.[18] Within four months the Board of Trade responded to Murray's vigorous plea and asked the Admiralty to draw up a plan for the establishment of a board.[19] Although the Board of Trade and the Admiralty continued to correspond in regard to a marine board, they took no action during 1844 and by 1845 the Board of Trade and Parliament were so busy with railway bills that they could no longer seriously consider the question.[20] During the next few years, Murray continued to advocate the establishment of a central board, but the question of the navigation acts and of free trade subverted the Government's attention. No comprehensive legislation was feasible until that issue was settled.

By the end of the forties the railway fever was over and the navigation acts had been repealed. Parliament was free to attend to other matters. The maritime code, discussed at length in Parliament during the debates on the Navigation Acts, demanded clarification. A comprehensive act would clear up inconsistencies among the provisions of the old acts and define the responsibilities of the Board of Trade as a board of shipping. It had become the recognized authority in practice, it was time it was so treated in law. The Act of 1850, the first comprehensive act, made clear that " the Board of Trade shall undertake the general superintendence of matters relating to the British merchant marine." [21] It was remarkably inclusive, yet it was the result of compromise and therefore had to be complemented by more acts during the next three years. It was only in 1854 that Parliament was ready to pass a really complete act. The great Merchant Shipping Act of 1854, consisting of 548 sections, finally defined the mercantile marine code, and did it so well that it remained substantially the authority into the twentieth century.

But preliminary to the consolidation acts of the fifties, there were the twenty years of legislation concerned with the many individual activities of the shipping industry. Firstly there were the problems of navigation : pilotage, lighthouses, the rules of the road and meteorology. Secondly there were all the questions related to the ships : their registry and tonnage measurement, the stowage of the cargoes, and the inspection of steamships and passenger ships. Thirdly there were the qualifications, discipline and supply of officers and seamen. And finally there were the matters related to human welfare : of the crews, the passengers, the coalwhippers, and those persons shipwrecked. Each was handled as a separate problem, and therefore each is more easily understood when described alone. A chronological account of the yearly growth of governmental regulation of shipping would be good if the process were not so confused. But so many different activities were treated independently by different men interested

in only one question, that the account would be as confusing as
the shipping code itself was before 1850. The final period, the
four years leading up to the act of 1850, consists of the simpler
history of consolidation and therefore can be accounted for
annually.

PILOTAGE

Of all the hazards of navigation, that of piloting, of sailing within
sight of land and of getting in and out of harbours was the most
dangerous. A ship well out to sea, if properly built and loaded,
and if well sailed, was safe. But one close to shore ran not only
all the usual risks, but had to be piloted carefully if it was not to
run aground. In the early nineteenth century, navigational aids
were crude as compared to those to-day. There were lighthouses,
beacons, and buoys, but they were inadequate and too infrequent.
With meteorology in its infancy, the frequent storms around the
British Isles came without warning, and made the lights or buoys
useless. On most coasts the harbours were few and spaced so far
apart that ships frequently were caught by storms too far from
port. But if a ship approached a port it still ran grave risks, for
the harbours were difficult to reach. For protection from piracy
and easy communication with the hinterland they had been
located well up rivers. Ships had to allow for river currents, for
the constant silting up and shifting of the channels, and also for
the tidal currents. A captain caught in conflicting tidal and river
currents in an unknown water was helpless. He must rely on a
pilot who was thoroughly familiar with local conditions.

By the eighteen-thirties much had been done to aid navigation
but the activity with the longest history was pilotage. The English
learned the value of pilots from the Spanish. Early in the sixteenth
century Charles the First (or Charles V of the Holy Roman
Empire) had established at Seville the Casa de Contratacion to
be the clearing house for all trade between Spain and the vast
new American empire. To train pilots in navigating ships the
long distance up the Guadalquivir River to Seville he established
at the Casa a school for pilots. Henry VIII followed the example
of his nephew and chartered the Trinity House of Deptford
Strond in Kent in 1515 to promote the commerce of his great
port of London by training and licensing pilots, and by erecting

lights and beacons on the Thames.[22] The immediate success of Trinity House in maintaining a ready supply of pilots in London led him to charter similar houses at Hull and Newcastle-upon-Tyne. Later other authorities were established, such as that of the Cinque Port Pilots along the English Channel, and still more recently at Bristol and the newer ports like Liverpool.

These authorities were chartered by the Government and in time were subjected to more and more comprehensive regulations. Rates were set, rules elaborated, and the qualifications of pilots were defined. The comprehensive act of 1808 authorized Trinity House of Deptford to appoint sub-commissioners of pilotage to qualify pilots for any area not already governed.[23] Trinity House, in fact, became the recognized senior authority, and co-operated closely with the Government in drawing up bills and in advising it on related matters. The department of the Government which dealt with Trinity House was the Board of Trade. In 1825, for example, in answer to proposals by Trinity House for clauses in a pilotage bill, the board " ordered that a letter be written to Mr. Herbert [the secretary of Trinity House] conveying their Lordships' approbation of the said proposal; and requesting that he will transmit the proposed clauses to this office as soon as may be practicable, when their Lordships will consider the whole of this subject and have a further communication with the corporation of Trinity House thereon, and will then take the necessary measures for submitting a bill to Parliament." [24] The increasing centralization of pilotage matters in Trinity House was complemented by the increasingly thorough supervision of Trinity House by the Board of Trade. The dual development has produced the modern administration of pilotage.

Yet the Board could not satisfy all the shipowners. They complained of excessively high dues, of the requirement that a pilot should be carried on ships like coastal traders when they did not think that he was necessary. The Board responded to one complaint in a typical manner. Its letter said " that the Lords of this Committee have not lost sight of this question, but that they have found the difficulties attending it too numerous and too complicated to admit of their coming to any specific opinion upon the subject; and that under these circumstances their lordships are glad to find that it is likely to become a matter of enquiry before a Committee of the House of Commons." [25]

Sooner or later the Government would respond to the shipowners' complaints in the usual way, that is, by the appointment
in 1836 of a royal commission of inquiry " to inquire into the laws
and regulations relating to Pilotage." [26] The commissioners pro-
ceeded with their inquiry on three principles. It was of very great
importance to the commercial marine that a sound and efficient
system of pilotage be maintained; it was expedient to effect the
utmost possible reduction in pilotage charges which might be
consistent with the prompt and efficient performance of their
duties; and the law should be made simple and perspicuous.
Since most complaints had been of details, the commissioners
offered various specific recommendations but decided that in
general the existing authorities were doing well. They did recommend that Parliament should pass a general public act which
would replace the many private acts, such act to establish a
uniform system of rules governing the 2,323 pilots of the whole
kingdom. Although each authority should have ample powers,
these should be well defined, and Trinity House should be the
ultimate authority. It should sanction all bylaws and rates and
be the source of appeal for all redress (rather than the Privy
Council which was generally not prepared to act effectively).
Also, Trinity House should appoint sub-commissioners to supervise all other authorities. No action was taken on the report
because the problem was not acute and no one was sufficiently
interested in reform.

In the same year, 1836, the Board of Trade made the first
decision toward solving the problem of whether or not steam
vessels should be exempt from pilot dues. Because of their motive
power, they were not so subject as were sailing vessels to tidal and
river currents and therefore should not pay as high dues. The
Board drew up the draft of the Order in Council which allowed
them a reduction of one-fourth in dues.

In the forties the problem of putting all pilots under Trinity
House came up several times. Should the Cinque Port pilots be
included with those of Trinity House? Their warden, the Duke
of Wellington, agreed that they should, but nothing was done.[27]
The committee of inquiry into the causes of shipwrecks in 1843
recommended that the Board of Trade should inspect all pilot
stations every three years, but again no change was made.[28] In

fact, no change was made until the consolidation acts of the
fifties. The private authorities continued to function, generally
supervised by Trinity House in close co-operation with the Board
of Trade.

LIGHTHOUSES

Another aid to navigation was the lighthouses around the coasts.
They had a history as old as that of pilots but by the early nineteenth century, the system of lighthouses was in an anarchic
state; they had been built from time to time, here and there, as
need arose or the capital was found to pay for their construction.
By 1835 there were over two hundred around the British Isles.[29]
They were controlled or operated by individual persons or groups
who owned the land upon which they were built or leased it from
the Crown. Since the amount of the dues charged ships which
had to pass the light was usually set by the owner of the light,
and since, even when fixed by the government, the dues were
high, lights were a profitable investment. There had always been
some objection to this system, but the eighteenth-century tradition
of private property had been too strong to allow any change in
it. However, by the early years of the nineteenth century, three
bodies had gained control of half of the lights : Trinity House of
Deptford, England; the Ballast Board of Dublin, Ireland; and
the Commissioners of Northern Lights, Scotland. The process
of consolidation had begun.

But with the increased amount of shipping, dissatisfaction with
the existing system became more vociferous each year. With
more and more shipwrecks and increased loss of life and property,
both the humanitarians and the shipowners were aroused. Added
to those groups were the mercantile interests who sought decreased
duties on trade. Since other countries generally maintained lights
on their coasts free of duties, or at least charged smaller duties
than the English, those members of the Government and their
allies among merchants who were trying to negotiate reciprocal
treaties were constantly asked to lower the duties charged by
British lighthouses. And foreigners, accustomed to a national and
rational system, were particularly sensitive to the exorbitant rates
of England and to her highly variable rules. Free-traders were
staunchly behind reform.

Probably the factor which made the reforming movement too strong to hold off was the growing realization on the part of the shipping interests that they were being robbed. Joseph Hume, that perennial economical reformer, in debate in the House of Commons, estimated that they were paying £240,000 in light dues when the upkeep of the lights cost only £99,000. With a little house-cleaning, their upkeep should cost only £40,000.[30] His figures may have been exaggerated, but the numerous merchants could hardly ignore his argument in their fight against the few lighthouse owners.

As early as 1822, a select committee of the House of Commons advised that all lighthouses should be put under the superintendence of Trinity House. But the recommendation was premature; the agitation for change had not yet produced sufficient feeling for reform. Twelve years later, in 1834, the commotion out-of-doors had become loud enough to produce another select committee. This committee was particularly strong and brought out an elaborate report which went into every detail of the whole problem of lighthouse administration. The report appealed to the humanitarians, for in it they said that they had " throughout been strongly impressed with the paramount necessity of having the best lighthouses ... for this great Naval and Commercial Country which the state of science can afford; and that every necessary expense should be incurred for their maintenance " for the safety of persons and property.[31] But the real blow to the *status quo* came when they said that :

They have found that these establishments, of such importance to the extensive naval and commercial interests of this Kingdom, instead of being conducted under the immediate superintendence of the government, upon one uniform system, and under responsible public servants, with proper foresight to provide for the safety of the shipping in the most efficient manner, and on the most economical plans, have been left to spring up, as it were, by slow degrees, as the local wants required, often after disastrous losses at sea; and it may, perhaps, be considered as matter of reproach to this great country, that for ages past, as well as the present time, a considerable portion of the establishments of lighthouses have been made the means of heavily taxing the trade of the country, for the benefit of a few private indivi-

duals, who have been favoured with that advantage by the
ministers and the sovereigns of the day.[32]

The committee recommended that all lighthouses in England,
Scotland, and Ireland should be placed under one board, resident
in London, and that they be conducted under one system of
management.

The next year, 1835, Joseph Hume introduced a bill to put
into effect the recommendations of the committee of which he
was the chairman. But the opposition was too strong and he was
forced to withdraw the bill. Among his opponents was the
Government, for it found itself in a rather embarrassing position.
As the landlord, it leased out to lighthouse operators land worth
£100,000 a year. The Commissioners of Woods and Forests did
not want to give up that handsome income, and furthermore,
those were the years when economical reforms were pressing
hardest on the Government and denying it enough income to carry
on essential services. The Government may have been overcharg-
ing shipowners but it had to try to hold on to its income.[33]

Again the next year Hume introduced his bill, demanding that
all lighthouses be supervised by the Government, for " what was
the Board of Trade for, if not to undertake the management of
such matters as this? "[34] The Government now had to give in,
and inducing Hume to withdraw his bill, they introduced their
own. Thomson, the President of the Board of Trade, presented
the bill. There was agreement that a central board should supervise all lighthouses, but the main part of the debate centred in
the question of whether Trinity House should assume that control,
or whether it should be the Admiralty. Hume and others
preferred the Admiralty, but Thomson answered, " If they were
to admit officers of the Navy, for instance, great interest might
be made by the Admiralty or some other power, for Captain A. or
Captain B., and he thought it better they should have as Members
of the Board, hard-working, practical men."[35] Admiral Sir
Edward Codrington, the victor of Navarino and now an ardent
follower of shipping legislation, argued in favour of the retention
of control by the Government. " He considered the speech of the
right hon. Gentleman, the President of the Board of Trade, as a
very mercantile speech altogether, and as advocating exclusive
sentiments not worthy of his station and character."[36] Thomson

was obviously bargaining for the support of shippers who much preferred Trinity House to any Government office. Thomson won out with the support of Sir Robert Peel, the leader of the Conservative group, and the bill was passed.[37] It gave control of all lights to Trinity House with the exception of those in Scotland and Ireland, which were to continue to be run by the Commissioners of Northern Lights, and the Ballast Board of Dublin. Those bodies were too strongly established to be pushed over by the Government yet, but to a certain extent they were held responsible to Trinity House.

The big step had been made; control had been largely centralized, and with the general close relationship between Trinity House and the Board of Trade, there was tacit supervision by the Government. The commission of inquiry of 1845, with Joseph Hume again as chairman, went into the subject of lighthouses in great detail, but came up with few new recommendations, except that one third of the Board of Trinity House should be nominated by the Government. In 1849 Labouchere, the President of the Board of Trade, tried to push a bill through Parliament to substitute for the inadequate and imperfect control over lighthouse authorities " an efficient control by a Government board of management." [38] He failed because local interests were too strong.

In the fifties, certain changes were made, the most significant being the transfer from the three local authorities of all funds to the Board of Trade. The consolidation acts in general increased the degree of control exercised by the Board of Trade.[39]

RULES OF THE ROAD

The administration of lights and pilots had been so well worked out by the fifties that even the revolutionary development of the steamship required little more by way of reform than some increased supervision by the Government and the use of technical improvements in lighting that were available. But the steamship did raise a problem that could not wait long to be solved. What were the rules of the road? [40] What were the conventions and laws which governed the right of way between two vessels meeting at sea? When all ships used sails for their motive power the Government did not have to define the rules because all ships obeyed well-known customs that were adequate. Slow-moving, offering high silhouettes so that they could be easily seen, sailing vessels approached each other so leisurely that their captains had enough time to ascertain the intention of the other and to take appropriate action to avoid collision.

The accepted convention as defined by Trinity House of Deptford was that the vessel close hauled had the right of way over the one sailing before the wind; that if two vessels met close hauled, the one on the starboard tack should have the right of way; and that when two vessels were sailing before the wind, both should put their helms to port and pass to port. Single white lights were to be shown when other vessels came near, and since bad visibility in fog meant no wind and vessels therefore were moving slowly or not at all (in case of currents captains frequently anchored), a bell rung occasionally did all that could be done by way of warning other ships. Those simple rules had been sufficient and there had been few losses of vessels due to collisions.

But with the rapidly increasing use of steam engines for propulsion, vessels moved faster, offered lower silhouettes, and were not slowed down by fog. Whereas sailing vessels could not sail directly into the wind, steam vessels were quite unrestricted as to their direction. All in all, the chances for confusion and collision were dramatically apparent. In the period 1848 and 1849 there were 3,064 collisions and 279 vessels were totally lost.

It was not until 1846 that any steps were taken to define the rules. The Steam Navigation Act of that year gave the Admiralty the responsibility of prescribing the lights steamships should carry.[41] Captain W. D. Evans had been advocating the use of running lights, red on the port side and green on the starboard, to be seen only from dead ahead to two points abaft the beam on the appropriate side. By 1848 the Admiralty was convinced of the utility of Evans's lights and ordered all steamships to show them together with a white masthead light visible from ahead over twenty points of the compass. With those lights two ships meeting at night could determine roughly what direction each was heading. From time to time Captain Evans was employed by the Admiralty at the naval dockyards to superintend the fitting of the lights. By the Steam Navigation Act the Board of Trade had received certain obligations for the inspection and safety of steam vessels and therefore was responsible for the fitting of lights on merchant vessels. Therefore, through its influence, Evans also assisted in their installation on those ships. Upon the Board's recommendation, the Treasury paid him £200 for his services. In 1850 the Admiralty paid him £500 and suggested that the Board pay him another £200. The Board agreed but the Treasury did not, so that the Admiralty gave him an additional £500. Meanwhile the Russian government gave him £200 and a gold watch.

The Board of Trade realized that sailing as well as steam vessels should carry lights and tried to persuade the Admiralty to issue the appropriate order. The Steam Navigation Act of 1851 gave the Admiralty the power, but that body considered that the customary lantern shown in an emergency was sufficient. It was only in 1858 that the Admiralty came around to the Board's opinion and prescribed lights for sailing vessels. The Merchant Shipping Amendment Act of 1862 made the Admiralty and the Board of Trade jointly responsible for the rules of the road.

METEOROLOGY

Navigation was made safer and more efficient by the increased number and the better design of lighthouses and lights, by the better supply of qualified pilots, and by the more careful observances of the recognized rules of the road; but still shipmasters had to take a chance on the weather. Although the location and track of a storm had to remain largely unknown until wireless telegraphy was in common use, less variable factors could be ascertained. By the systematic collection and evaluation of meteorological and hydrographical data, experts trained in those sciences could learn the general frequency and pattern of storms in any area, the behaviour of winds and currents, and could discover any natural phenomena of interest to shipmasters. By the eighteen-thirties the weather or sea had received little attention. Only the obvious had long been known : that sailing in the North was dangerous in the winter, that the Gulf Stream and the trade winds followed certain courses. But after 1830 the increased international competition among shipowners, the use of ships in winter, the concern for safety at sea, and economical navigation gradually aroused interest in the two sciences. The utility of the study of meteorology and hydrography was accepted by shipowners and the Government only after ten years of determined effort on the part of a few men. Perhaps the single most dramatic illustration of the value of the studies and certainly most convincing to shipowners came as a result of the discovery of gold in California. In their race to get there first, or to make more round trips from the east coast of the United States, shipmasters used the new charts, which included information about currents and winds, to such advantage that their sailing time was cut from 180 to 133 days.

Meanwhile the Hydrographic Office of the Admiralty, set up in 1795, despite its small budget of £650 a year, had carried out extensive surveys of coasts in many parts of the world, and increased the number of naval charts from 347 to 962 by 1830. It published its first official catalogue of charts that same year and two years later published the first official tide tables. Meanwhile it started the first systematic attempt to collect meteorological observations at sea. And in 1838, largely as a result of the publication of Sir William Reid's *An Attempt to Develop the Law of Storms*, in which he made a significant contribution to the circular theory of hurricanes, the Hydrographic Office requested officers of the Royal Engineers on detached stations and consuls in foreign ports to collect and send in meteorological information.

Reid continued to advocate the study of weather, but another Englishman became more famous. Captain Robert Fitzroy, a grandson of the Duke of Grafton and a descendant of Charles II, was given command of the brig *Beagle* and sent to survey the coasts of Patagonia and the Straits of Magellan. His trip was considered so successful that after a short visit to England in 1830 he was ordered to resume his survey, this time on a much more extensive scale. He took along as naturalist one of the most famous men of the century. On the recommendation of the Professor of Botany at Cambridge, Henslow, Charles Darwin reported aboard and was assigned to share the captain's cabin. For five years Fitzroy and Darwin cruised along the coasts of South America and around the world. Although Darwin's publications eventually became far more famous than those of his captain, Fitzroy published in 1839 a several-volume account of the voyage, one of which Darwin wrote. Fitzroy had long been interested in meteorology, and his detailed accounts of its importance on his voyage did much to draw attention to it. Sir Francis Beaufort, the leading hydrographer of the day, later said that " from the Equator to Cape Horn, and from thence round to the River Plata on the eastern side of America, all that is immediately wanted has been already achieved by the splendid survey of Captain Robert Fitzroy." [42] Back in England after 1836 Fitzroy remained a strong advocate of the scientific study of the weather around the world. Like many of his contemporaries he realized the value of the argument for economy. He wrote :

> The maritime commerce of the nations having been extended over the world to an unprecedented degree, and competition having reached such a point that the value of cargoes and profits of enterprise depended more than ever on the duration and nature of voyages, it was obviously a question of the greatest importance to determine the best tracks for ships to follow in order to make the quickest as well as the safest passages. The employment of steamers in such numbers, the prevalent endeavours to keep as near the direct line between two places (the arc of a great circle) as intervening obstacles, currents and winds allowed and the general improvement in navigation, caused a demand for more precise and readily available information respecting all frequented parts of the ocean. [43]

Meanwhile Lieutenant Matthew Maury of the United States Navy, with persistent effort, had persuaded the Navy and the Government to give him their support in his methodical study of wind and sea. He, too, had started his career with long voyages and surveys, one of which was around the world, and in 1836 had published *A New Theoretical and Practical Treatise on Navigation*. By 1842 he was recognized as head of a department of the Navy for the drawing of charts and other aids to navigation which should include the new information. With the publication of his wind and current chart of the North Atlantic in 1847, and other charts and information, Maury became famous. The English eventually realized the value of the new studies, and in 1851 suggested to the American government that the two countries co-ordinate their observations. The English, with extensive naval stations and more widespread merchant services, could complement the American observations. Maury, realizing the advantage of having one system of observation instead of many, quickly agreed and the conference met at Brussels in August 1853. The most famous delegate was, of course, Lieutenant Maury. Those for England were Captain Beechey, one of the marine officers of the Board of Trade, and Captain Henry James of the Royal Engineers. Beechey, soon to become a Rear-Admiral, had carried out extensive surveys and was a famous geographer who long had known the value of these studies. Whereas Maury thought that the information should be for naval vessels, Beechey argued the importance of having all merchant vessels, the many thousands in all parts of the world, collect information too. Representing the greatest merchant marine in the world, he knew the importance of his plan. He succeeded in carrying the conference with him, and they went on to draw up sample logs to be kept by all ships, and to outline methods of observation and other details. The long report of the conference was the work of Maury and Beechey together.

In 1854 the Board of Trade informed the Royal Society that it planned to authorize the establishment of a Meteorological Office. In 1855 the office was set up with Fitzroy as chief, to be assisted by two officers, a draftsman, and three clerks.[44] Parliament voted £3,200 for its support and the Admiralty gave another £1,000. The Board of Trade had no authority but it did act as liaison between the office and the merchant ships. Another result of the almost illegitimate origins of the office is suggested by the source of Fitzroy's salary. He received £300 from the Admiralty and another £300 from the Board of Trade.

The great problem in respect to getting the merchant vessels to take observations was the objection of shipowners to buying the necessary instruments.[45] The Board of Trade, in contrast to the Admiralty, could not afford to give them to shipowners; it could merely encourage shipowners to buy and install the instruments. It did delegate agents at ports to instruct shipmasters in the use of the instruments when they were on board and to keep proper logs. By 1857, however, only about 200 merchant vessels had been fitted. Fitzroy carried on as head of the office until his death in 1865. He instituted a system of storm warnings and issued the first weather forecasts. His able and persistent contribution to the study of meteorology and hydrography remains another of the remarkable accomplishments of the early Victorians.

The Board of Trade was accused of injuring the merchant shipping industry by opening up all trade to foreign competition. But it helped the industry by improving the various aids to navigation. As the department of the Government charged with the general supervision of pilotage and lighthouses, it regularized their administration, encouraged their technical improvement, and standardized the fees charged for their services. It also worked to obtain the general acceptance of rules of the road adequate to steamship navigation, and co-operated with the Admiralty in the study and dissemination of meteorological data. The industry had reason to be grateful to the Board.

The growing concern of society and the Government for the general conditions in industry was further reflected by the other responsibilities acquired by the Board. Registration, supervision, and inspection were becoming the order of the day; and merchant shipping, one of the most complex of industries, was to be treated in a way similar to mining, manufacturing, and housing. Thus, the Board became involved with the registration of merchant ships, the measurement of their tonnage, with the inspection of steamships, and the methods of cargo stowage. It further became responsible for the welfare of various kinds or classes of persons involved with shipping. All the duties of the Board were finally defined in the great Consolidation Act of 1854. Before that the Board tended to treat each as a separate problem. It is best for the historian to follow suit.

SHIPS' REGISTRY

As early as 1660 the Navigation Acts limited trade between two ports governed by England to ships owned by Englishmen. To establish that ownership and thus to enjoy the privilege ships had to be registered at the port where they were owned. Once a ship was registered at the Customs House of that port, the customs officer who maintained the register issued a certificate which was kept on board at all times so that upon arrival in a port, the shipmaster might prove that the ship was English and enjoy the advantages of trading there. Three departments of the Government were very much concerned with ships' registry: the Admiralty was responsible for backing up the customs officer who registered the ships; the Treasury, relying heavily upon customs revenue, was crucially concerned for the rules of registry and their maintenance; and the Board of Trade was generally responsible for the composition of the Registry Acts and their passage through Parliament. The Board also acted as the intermediary between shipowners and other departments of the Government.

Two acts passed in 1824 and 1826 regulated the rules of registry for the middle years of the nineteenth century.[46] They prescribed the registration form, or certificate. It was to include the vessel's name, its tonnage, the place of construction, the port to which it belonged, the names of the owners and the shipmaster (the acts defined what persons were qualified to register ships), and the particulars of the ship's build—its dimensions, number of decks, and kind of rigging. Although John Herries, then financial secretary to the Treasury, presented the second bill to Parliament, Huskisson as the President of the Board of Trade piloted both bills through the House of Commons.

The provisions of the acts remained substantially the same throughout the period. From time to time shipowners petitioned the Government for specific changes in the provisions, but agreement among the owners and the various departments of the Government concerned as to what those reforms should be, was impossible. For instance, a bill proposed by the Board of Trade in 1835 was dropped as the result of the opposition to many of its clauses by the General Shipowners' Society.[47]

A long act in 1845 reviewed the provisions for registry and added others to include the registration of steam vessels.[48] In 1854 the Consolidation Act gave complete responsibility for the composition and the superintendence of the provisions to the Board of Trade.

TONNAGE MEASUREMENT

A vessel's tonnage was the measurement of its carrying capacity or burden. In the fifteenth century a ton meant the space occupied by a tun or cask of wine so that a ship of so many tons was assumed to carry that number of tuns of wine. Governmental taxation of the ship or of its cargo was based on the tonnage of the ship, but also other dues or fees came to be so based. A ship had to pay to pass by lighthouses, to anchor in or use a harbour, or to come alongside a pier, and to use the services of a pilot. Thus one of the first specifications listed on a ship's certificate of registry was its tonnage.

The relationship between a ship's size and the number of tons it carried remained in name only. Various rules for measurement dating back to 1422 had long since been substituted for the original ton.[49] But the rules of measurement prescribed in 1773 to apply to all classes of ships and still in force in the eighteen-twenties were as follows : to measure the length and the breadth of the ship in a specific manner, then, to subtract three-fifths of the breadth from the length, multiply the result by the breadth, multiply that product by one-half the breadth, and divide the product by ninety-four. The quotient was the measure of the ship's tonnage.[50]

The evils of this method were well known. Since the depth of a ship was not measured at all and the breadth was such an important factor, owners ordered ships that were too deep for their breadth. They also resorted to certain devices in construction which reduced the measurement of the length and the breadth of the ship. The result was that the shipowner might register a ship at only three-fifths of its real tonnage and thus save two-fifths in dues and taxes, but it also encouraged the use of unseaworthy ships.[51] During the French wars, while ships were badly needed, ship losses could be excused, and all ships sailed in slow convoy, the evil remained unnoticed, but with peace, and the resumption of independent sailing and the revival of competition, the bad sailing qualities of English ships were revealed.

In 1820, at the request of the Board of Trade, the Admiralty appointed a commission to inquire into tonnage measurement.[52] Their inquiries exposed the evils of the existing system, but the members could not agree on any plan whereby the mathematical accuracy of measurement could be ensured. They did suggest using the weight of the cargo as a means of measurement, the amount to be determined by the difference between the marks on the hull made by the water when the ship was empty and when it was loaded; but that raised the difficult problem of who was to decide how much a ship might safely carry. (Fifty years later Plimsoll knew that he had the answer.) Furthermore, light and pilot dues were charged not only according to the weight of the cargo but also that of the ship. Their report was ignored; customs officers continued to measure ships according to the old rules.

During the twenties, there was little progress, but by the thirties the Admiralty and the Board of Trade agreed that some changes had to be made. In 1831, with the Board's endorsement, the Admiralty set William Parsons to work investigating a new method of measurement. He received reports from foreign countries on their rules and recommendations from the outports. The Board of Trade followed his investigation closely.[53] After two years of good work but no ready solution, the Board of Trade requested the Admiralty to appoint another committee to inquire into " the best mode " of measuring tonnage. Davies Gilbert, who had sat on the committee of 1820, was now joined by Captain Beaufort, the famous hydrographer of the Admiralty, and others. In February of 1834 the committee reported that tonnage should be a measure of the internal capacity of a ship as before but now determined by measuring all enclosed or interior spaces, and not by a formula based on the two simple measurements of the length and the breadth. By measuring all the enclosed volume ship-owners would no longer be induced to build unseaworthy ships because now there would be no advantage in following faulty dimensions. The engine room of a steamship was not to count as an enclosed space. The appropriate bill was prepared and after the Board of Trade, the Treasury, the Commissioners of Customs, the Admiralty and private interests had agreed on its details, it was presented to Parliament in August of 1835. Francis Baring, a joint secretary of the Admiralty, presented the bill, but it was Thomson, the President of the Board of Trade, who was really responsible for both the provisions of the bill and for its passage. The precedent established by this Act of determining tonnage by the total enclosed volume was so sound in principle that it remains operative to-day.[54] However, it was to be over twenty years before the new rules were to be accepted for all shipowners. Firstly, the great number of owners of ships built according to the old rules stoutly refused to accept any rules of measurement of an *ex post facto* nature. Many owners were strongly opposed to the new rules for other reasons. And, furthermore, the Government hesitated to enforce the new rules because the method of measuring interior spaces was not completely clear. Those spaces were often of such peculiar shapes that the customs officers did not know how to measure them.

To clarify the situation, the shipowners persuaded the Board of Trade to request the Admiralty to appoint another committee of inquiry in 1849. The committee, presided over by Lord John Hay, one of the Lords of the Admiralty, reported that tonnage should be based on the entire cubic contents of the vessels measured externally. But the prejudice by now against external measurement was so great that the bill introduced in 1850 including the recommendations of the committee was quietly dropped.

G. Moorsom, the secretary to this committee, continued to try to solve the problem of internal measurement. By 1854 he had worked out a feasible method and convinced the Board of Trade of its utility so that in the great act of consolidation of that year they incorporated his rule. These provisions established the rule that the internal volume was to be divided by one hundred, and each hundred cubic feet of space was to be called, for convenience, a ton. Gross tonnage was to include all enclosed areas, whereas register tonnage was to exclude certain areas used for fuel, engines and the crew. A dispute over what areas or how much space should be excluded went on for years. Moorsom was appointed to the position of Surveyor General of Tonnage in 1855 at a salary of £800. Although the responsibility for measurement remained with the customs until 1872 when it was transferred to the Board of Trade, the latter was in effect responsible for the rules of its measurement during that period. It was, of course, the Board which bore the brunt of Plimsoll's attack in the seventies.

STEAMSHIP INSPECTION

Although steam engines had occassionally been used for the propulsion of ships during the eighteenth century, it was only in the early years of the nineteenth that they were used successfully. With the *Charlotte Dundas*, built in Scotland in 1802, and the *Clermont*, built in the United States in 1807 (but using an English engine), the steamship became commercially useful, and in the following years more and more ships were built to be propelled by steam. Their great advantage over sailing ships was their speed

and their ability to maintain schedules, for they were not
dependent upon uncertain or non-existent winds. By the twenties
they were used on many mail services where regular sailings were
desired. They were also most commonly used as tugs to tow
sailing ships in or out of harbours, and as inland excursion
steamers for passengers. Whereas in 1817 there were only 14
steam vessels, with a total tonnage of 1,039, operating in Great
Britain, in 1836 there were 554, of 59,362 tons, and in 1843 there
were 855 of 109,288 tons.[55] Yet with all its advantages, the steamship did not surpass the sailing ship in number or tonnage until
about 1870.

It suffered from several disadvantages. For propulsion it used
paddle-wheels which were unreliable because they were too
fragile. They were often smashed in storms, or in docking. It was
only after the fifties that an efficient propeller became common.[56]
But a more important disadvantage was in the inefficiency of the
engine itself. It weighed too much, took up too much space and
burned too much fuel. The combined space and weight of the
machinery and fuel reduced the space available for cargo. Therefore until the sixties and seventies when more efficient machinery
was developed, steamships were used primarily as tugs, and for
carrying mail and passengers on short trips. For carrying cargoes
at sea or for any distance the sailing vessel had to be used.

But the use of steam entailed a disadvantage of particular
concern to those aboard a steamship. The steam, which was raised
to high pressure, did not always reach the piston; sometimes it
blew up the boiler first. The problem of disciplining steam
undoubtedly had its excitement, but it also had its deaths. More
and more men were killed every year. By 1817 the reaction to
this idiosyncrasy become so pronounced, that it could no longer
be ignored. A select committee of the House of Commons was
appointed " to consider of the means of preventing the mischief
of explosion from happening on board Steam Boats, to the danger
or destruction of His Majesty's Subjects on board such Boats." [57]
The committee introduced its recommendations with the comfort-
ing statement to the House of Commons that :

[They] entered on the task assigned them, with a strong feeling
of the inexpediency of legislative interference with the manage-

ment of private concerns or property, farther than the public safety should demand, and more especially with the exertions of that mechanical skill and ingenuity, in which the artists of this country are so pre-eminent, by which the labour of man has been greatly abridged, the manufactures of the country carried to an unrivalled perfection, and its commerce extended over the whole world.

Despite its general opposition to any legislative measure by which " the science and ingenuity of our artists might appear to be fettered or discouraged," the committee, in the face of the rising number of boiler murders, recognized certain measures which should be taken for public safety. It recommended that passenger steam vessels be registered at the nearest port, that boilers be made of wrought iron or copper, that they be inspected, that they have two safety valves, one to be inaccessible to the engine man, that boilers be inspected for their strength, and that there be penalties for putting weights on valves. But the ministry was preoccupied and hardly noticed the report; boilers continued to blow up in alarming profusion.

At the instance of Colonel Sibthorpe, the famous ultra-tory, another select committee was appointed in 1831. Concerned more with the whole problem of steam navigation than with that associated with boilers, the committee recommended various safety devices for all steamships, and particularly advised the survey of all steamships for seaworthiness.[58] *The Times* hoped that the Government would not be content with just the inquiry; but again, legislation was put off.

During the thirties the destruction of lives and property continued, together with the agitation for some kind of Governmental action. Articles in newspapers and journals reported and described wrecks, and many persons published their plans for reform. Whistles were suggested, new rules of the road were drawn up, and owners tried new devices such as installing the helm in the forward part of the ship so that the helmsman had better visibility. But accidents continued and in those ten years, ninety-two steamships were lost with 634 lives. By 1839 the Board of Trade responded to the growing demand for another inquiry and appointed Captain R. E. Pringle and Josiah Parker to investigate the causes of steamboat accidents and to recommend means for preventing their occurrence.[59] They recommended that the Board of Trade institute a system of periodical survey, and that all steam vessels should be licensed. A special board should be set up under the Board of Trade to register and classify all vessels according to their build and specifications, to appoint local and district surveyors, to investigate accidents, and to report annually to Parliament.[60] The Board, accepting their suggestions, requested William Page Wood (later Lord Hatherley, the Lord Chancellor) to prepare the appropriate bill.[61] Henry Labouchere, the President of the Board of Trade, introduced the bill in the next session of Parliament but the opposition was very strong and since he was not really convinced that legislation was necessary, he was readily persuaded that the bill should be dropped.[62]

But the memorials in favour of Government action continued to remind the Board of Trade of its responsibility. The inquiry into the causes of shipwreck in 1843 again recommended the placing of all steam vessels under the supervision of the Government.[63] Despite the strong opposition of the General Association of Proprietors of Steam Shipping, the Board realized that legislation was appropriate, and the Vice-President, Sir George Clerk, introduced and carried a bill for the regulation of steam navigation in 1846.[64] Among other responsibities the Board was to appoint inspectors who were to survey all steam vessels for the " sufficiency and condition of the hull " and of the machinery, and to issue certificates of registry. Customs officers were not to clear ships without the certificates. All accidents were to be reported to the Board. It appointed a naval officer, Captain Denham, to set up and administer the new Steam Navigation Department.[65] In May 1847 the Board issued the list of approved surveyors. Fees were charged for surveying each ship.

By 1848 the Marine Department and the surveying of ships were running smoothly except that a few ships continued to evade the survey. Therefore the Board secured another act which fined shipowners ten shillings a day for every day the report of a survey was late. It furthermore gave the inspectors the power to determine the number of passengers a steam vessel should carry.[66] Another act in 1851 gave the Board further powers, and the Consolidation Act of 1854 further defined the Board's function. Nevertheless, it was the Act of 1846 which set the precedent for the later development.

CARGO STOWAGE

The kind of cargo and the method of its stowage were often important reasons for the loss of ships. Timber ships were the most obvious examples, for they were notorious for the large loads they carried on deck and their subsequent unseaworthiness. The big demand for timber, especially in the thirties, greatly increased the number of ships used in that trade. There was not only the conflict between the merchants bringing timber from British North America, who were given special protection since the wars with France, and the merchants who wanted to bring timber from the Baltic but who were discriminated against by the trade Acts; but also the conflict between most merchants who wanted no restrictions as to how they should transport timber, and the reformers who realized that many losses at sea were due to faulty stowage. Because timber was of light bulk and awkward shapes, the custom was to stow much of it on deck, which means that in stormy weather the vessel was prone to become topheavy and founder. Furthermore, vessels were often used in the North American timber trade when they were no longer fit for other trades. The investigating committees of 1836 and 1839 both recommended restrictions as to the loading of timber. In this case the number of operators affected was small and their guilt was manifest so that the President of the Board of Trade had little difficulty in steering through Parliament the Acts of 1839 and the renewal Acts which forbade deck cargoes during winter months and restricted the amount of cargo at other times.[67] The success of these Acts was attested by the decline in the number of lives lost from an annual average of 306 in the years 1833 to 1835; to 106, 1840 to 1842, and the number of ships from 56 to 23. Finally, as a result of the Plimsoll agitation, all timber cargoes on deck were forbidden.

The first enactment, so far as the Board of Trade was concerned, dealing with the carriage of highly inflammable and explosive goods like gunpowder was in the Act of 1854. This put a penalty of £100 on any person who sent any dangerous goods aboard ship without the knowledge of the master. Furthermore, the master or owner had the right to refuse to accept any goods suspected of being dangerous.

While the Board was given increasing supervision of the construction and registration of ships, the machinery of steamships, and the stowage of cargoes, it was also given certain responsibilities for the persons associated with the shipping industry. Shipmasters were to be properly qualified for command. Seamen were to be registered, disciplined, and properly treated. Passengers and coal-whippers were to be protected. Since the new duties were acquired independently of one another, they are best described in a similar manner.

SHIPMASTERS

Improving navigational aids and compelling owners to sail more seaworthy ships helped reduce the number of ship losses, but even more crucial reforms were those concerned with the men who manned the ships. The need for more qualified personnel was desperate. The seamen were drunken, undisciplined and irrespon-sible; the officers, unqualified. And as the merchant marine grew larger, the quality of its personnel deteriorated.

Although the only qualification imposed on ships' personnel by the Government had been that of the navigation Acts, which required that the shipmaster and a large proportion of the crew should be of British nationality, their quality had been higher before the nineteenth century. Navigation schools had helped to train the masters, but the reason for the previous higher quality of the marine had been the ample supply of middle and upper class men who had entered the service.[68] The fleet had been smaller, the rewards greater and the profession honourable. Many younger sons of the gentry and the commercial classes had gone to sea. They had some education and took pride in their profession. By the eighteen-thirties many of the available ships' officers were men of less background and less intelligence. Their pay was insufficient, their employers in a depressed state, and their pro-fession less respected. Although the East India Company and some of the other larger shipowners could afford to maintain high standards, the majority of the smaller owners hired whatever officers they could find.[69] Any qualifications beyond that of nationality were out of the question. As a result it was estimated that one half of the growing number of shipwrecks were caused by incapable shipmasters.

The select committee which inquired into the causes of ship-wreck in 1836 found that two of the ten main causes of shipwreck

were the incompetency of masters and mates and the drunkenness of officers and men. Therefore, among their recommendations were the examination of officers, the establishment of
nautical schools for younger apprentices, and various provisions
to do with seamen. Furthermore, they recommended that an
inquiry be held in the case of every wreck and that if the shipmaster were found negligent, he be suspended from duty.[70] The
bill introduced the next year (1837) by Buckingham intended to
realize the recommendations of this committee was easily defeated
by the shipowners. But the inquiry had advertised the sorry state
of the marine and encouraged criticism of shipmasters. Henceforth the agitation for the qualification of officers increased each
year. Letters were written and motions introduced in Parliament.
Again the Government realized that conditions were not good,
but it was confused as to how the examinations should be under-
taken. The President of the Board of Trade in his speech against
the Act of 1837 had suggested that the Trinity House should
institute voluntary examinations. Some shipowners and associa-
tions set their own examinations but in the industry there was
wide disagreement as to the right procedure. How could the
Board of Trade resolve the conflicting opinions of all the owners,
who sailed many different kinds of ships in as many different
services? Comparisons with France, which held examinations
and maintained higher standards, were considered irrelevant
because her marine was so much smaller.

In 1840 the Glasgow underwriters sent a memorial to the Board
of Trade for the establishment of a marine board for the examination of ships' officers. The General Shipowners' Society was
itself so disunited on the issue that it could reach no decision as
to its attitude towards the request. The Board of Trade reflected
the prevailing dispute when it replied that " highly as they prized
these exertions of the Glasgow Association and other public bodies
for the improvement of the character of British seamen, their
lordships are not prepared to sanction a measure so general in its
application as the one proposed in this memorial. That their lordships indeed see very great, if not insuperable, difficulties in framing
any measure of the kind with a fair prospect of success, and that
under such circumstances they are not disposed to take up the
question at present." [71]

The Glasgow underwriters, as well as others, continued to press for examinations. The General Shipowners' Society, by 1841, had set itself against the movement because it might lead to the inexpedient interference with the rights of private judgment in the management of private property. The same year the famous meteorologist, Captain Fitzroy, became a leader of the movement and circulated throughout the the kingdom the draft of a bill he proposed to introduce for the examination of officers. While the Board of Trade politely acknowledged a copy of Fitzroy's bill, the favourable reaction in the outports was quite outspoken.[72] At a public meeting at Liverpool in January of 1842, attended by shipmasters, mates, and others, the following memorial was drawn up and sent to the President of the Board of Trade :

> The memorialists begged to call the attention of the Board of Trade to the lamentable loss of life and property annually occurring by shipwreck, and to the indisputable fact that many of such disasters at sea were attributable to the incompetency of those placed in charge of merchant vessels; and the object of the memorialists was to submit to the Board of Trade the necessity of requiring that all masters and mates should have passed an examination.[73]

Favourable memorials were received from many societies such as the Directors of the Liverpool Marine Assurance Company, the Liverpool East India and China Association, the Shipowners of Dumbarton, the Trinity House at Leith, the Shipowners of Aberdeen, and the Glasgow East India Association. Few were received against the bill. The Board meanwhile co-operated with Fitzroy in working out the clauses of his bill.[74]

The next year, 1843, the committee of the House of Commons selected to inquire into the causes of shipwrecks recommended, as did its predecessor, that local boards should examine the qualifications of masters and mates.[75] Meanwhile Fitzroy had introduced his bill, but before it could come up for debate he was appointed Governor of New Zealand, and with his abrupt departure from the House, the bill was dropped. Fitzroy's work had not been all in vain, for he had aroused strong feeling and, at the same time, James Murray of the Foreign Office was circulating the reports that he was collecting from the overseas consuls illustrating the inferior state of the merchant marine. The next year Gladstone, who had become President of the Board of Trade, realized something should be done. He wrote a letter to the chairman of the committee for managing the affairs of *Lloyd's Register* ... of shipping requesting that committee's co-operation in regard to pointing out in their annual register those masters and mates who have undergone voluntary examination.[76] Lloyd's enthusiastically promised their co-operation, and so Gladstone wrote to the Admiralty asking them to prepare a plan :

(1) for the formation of an adequate number of Boards in London and outports to conduct the proposed examinations;
(2) for the division of the certificates into classes, according to the standard of proficiency, and for the specification of the subjects of examination according to the functions to be performed;
(3) for defining the conditions with respect to which and knowledge or conduct under which certificates are to be annulled.[77]

The Liverpool Registry of Shipping promised its co-operation.[78] Meanwhile the Admiralty and the Board of Trade decided to include in the Merchant Seamen's Registry Bill, which was being drawn up at the Board, appropriate clauses for the examination of officers.[79] But the Government withdrew its clauses and the bill was presented without the provisions. The Board of Trade substituted its original plan for voluntary examinations. In 1845 it drew up an Order in Council outlining the regulations whereby Trinity House and the sub-commissioners of pilotage were to conduct the examinations. The various local boards were then to send in reports to the Board of Trade which would publish the names and particulars of each officer in the *Gazette* and would inform *Lloyd's Register* so that it too would publish the names.[80] The Board assumed that the advantage to each master of having his qualifications known would be sufficient to encourage them to take the examinations. And, in fact, by the end of 1850 over 3,000 shipmasters had been gazetted.[81]

SEAMEN'S REGISTRY

In an Act passed in 1835 Parliament stated that " the Prosperity,

Strength, and Safety of [the kingdom] principally depend on a large, constant, and ready Supply of Seamen, as well for carrying on the Commerce as for the Defence Thereof, and that it is therefore necessary to aid by all practicable Means, the increase of the Number of such Seamen, and to give them all due Encouragement and Protection." [82]   This Act was intended to consolidate the many previous acts which had long regulated the supply of seamen.   As part of the structure of the seventeenth-century navigation Acts, the shipowners agreed with the Government that in return for trading privileges and monopolies in the Empire, they would act as a source of seamen for the Royal Navy. Thus the owners were to man their ships primarily with British subjects, to carry apprentices and to meet the other requirements of the Admiralty as to the treatment and training of their crews. During the eighteenth century this arrangement worked tolerably well, but after 1792 with the awful strain of the long twenty years of war against France, the Navy's appetite for seamen could not be satisfied from any source.   To get more and more sailors, it abused its old right of impressment to the extent of sending the notorious press-gangs all over England, of seizing its reputed deserters from British merchant vessels, and from those of foreign nations.   Largely as a result of this practice the United States declared war on Great Britain in 1812.[83]   The problem was soon solved by the defeat of France in 1814, and the drastic reduction in the size of the Navy.[84]

But retrenchment supposes security, and by the thirties Englishmen were less complacent.   Growing world trade meant that the Navy had to protect more and more distant trading factories and colonies.   The French entry into Algeria in 1830, the Greek War of Independence, and the defeat of Turkey threatened the English domination of the Mediterranean.   And just across the channel the French were threatening war over Belgian independence.   In the circumstances, Sir James Graham, as First Lord, was able to effect some reforms at the Admiralty.   Certainly any thorough-going changes were impossible in those economical times, but consolidation of the laws governing the supply of seamen was possible.   Graham introduced the bill in 1834 but there was sufficient disagreement on details to have it put off until the next year.   Introduced again, it passed with little opposition.[85] The many provisions of the Merchant Seamen's Act were drawn up not only to keep account of the supply of seamen but also to ensure their welfare. Shipmasters were not to take seamen aboard without the latter's voluntary written agreement. The master was to give a discharged seaman a certificate. There were regulations about the payment of seamen, their treatment on board, and the adjudication of seamen's complaints by justices of the peace. It provided for the carrying of apprentices, and most important of all, it set up an office at the Customs House where a registrar was to keep a registry of all seamen. That official would thus have a constant record of the number of seamen available, would know their whereabouts, and have some information as to their past experience. The Admiralty would then not have to rely upon the press-gang. This was the first national register of labour and the first official case of directed labour.

The Admiralty, responsible for the administration of the Act, appointed Lieutenant J. H. Brown to be the first Registrar. Brown, put on half-pay in 1816 and despairing of full-time employment, after careful research wrote a report on the supply of seamen and the manning of ships. Graham had noticed this report and had recommended Brown's appointment to his successor, Sir Charles Wood. The office was set up at the Customs House in July 1835. Brown, paid a salary of £400, was given one assistant and four clerks.

Like so much of the legislation of these years, this Act met with various objections. The select committee which inquired into the causes of shipwreck in 1836 recommended that the registry include a clear description of the character of seamen so that those of better character would be favoured in getting jobs. Others joined in the criticism; consuls stationed in foreign ports continued to complain of the bad behaviour of British crews, and the various shipowners' societies objected to certain provisions. The most wholesale condemnation came from the General Ship-owners' Society at their meeting in April of 1839. Their com-mittee said:

From the period of passing the Merchant Seamen's Act your Committee have not ceased to receive representation of the utter inadequacy of the measures for the attainment of its avowed objects, and of the increasing evils arising from the impossibility of maintaining efficient discipline on board ships engaged in the

Merchant Service. So strongly, indeed, are your Committee impressed with the conviction, that unless some remedy be applied to this formidable and growing evil, consequences of the most disastrous to the interests of Commerce, and thence to British Naval Supremacy, must ensue, that they would have felt it their duty to have recommended an instant and urgent application for legislative interposition, were they not deterred by the recollection of the false principles and erroneous notions under which that interposition was exercised, when the Act now under review was, in the year 1835, introduced into Parliament. It was on that occasion the irksome task of many Members of your present Committee vainly to oppose those errors, to defend the Ship-owners against the unfounded charges brought against them as a class; and, unable to succeed in obtaining such provisions as their experience led them to be convinced were indispensable for the due regulation of the Merchant Service, it was only left them to predict the failure, which your Committee have now to deplore. But they greatly fear that the delusion which prevailed, when the question was last discussed in Parliament, has not yet passed away, and they feel that until the evil consequences of the present defective and objectionable system are forced by experience on the knowledge of the Admiralty and of the Naval Members of the House of Commons, any attempt at interference, on the part of Ship-Owners, which only expose them to a renewal of mortification and defeat, and probably to the introduction of some still more objectionable measure. Meantime on behalf of the Ship-Owners, they emphatically disclaim all desire to impose on our brave Seamen any harsh or unnecessary restraint,—their object being at once to protect the Sailor from injustice and tyranny, and to extend to those who are entrusted with the charge of Navigation, the means of maintaining that efficient discipline, without which neither commercial enterprise can be successfully conducted, nor safety be insured to property or to person in distant Navigation.

Generally the Act was successful and by 1842 there were over 258,000 seamen on the Register. But two years later the inevitable amending Act was passed.[86] It was prepared under the direction of the Admiralty, but its provisions were carefully reviewed by the Board of Trade.[87] Sidney Herbert, the secretary to the Admiralty, pointed out that the Act followed the general principles of that of 1835 but included certain alterations to make it more effective.[88]

Among the innovations were provisions for the protection of British seamen in cases where their ship might be sold in a foreign port. They were to be sent home at the expense of the owner. There were various provisions concerning food and medicines, including one which prescribed the daily serving of lime-juice as an antiscorbutic. Despite continued objections, this Act remained in effect until the consolidation acts of the fifties, when the responsibility for the registration of seamen was taken away from the Admiralty and given to the Board of Trade. Meanwhile the latter continued to advise.

However, Brown was given one other responsibility. The use of agents to sign up and furnish seamen to shipmasters had developed in recent years into a useful method of furnishing the captains a ready supply of sailors, but these agents, called crimps, had resorted to practices similar to those of the old press-gangs. They illegally impressed and kidnapped men who were drunk, and any others unfortunate enough to get into their clutches. The Board of Trade realized that the only necessary reform was an act which should provide for their registration. Their behaviour was so notorious that the Act was passed with little opposition.[89] The Act gave the Board the power to set up an office which would license such persons as they might deem requisite and fit " to hire, engage, supply, or provide seamen " to enter on board merchant ships. The Board and the Admiralty agreed that the Registrar of Seamen could assume this additional responsibility, and the Board paid him an extra £100 annually for his work of registering the crimps.[90] Once registered, the Board was able to track down any crimp who took advantage of seamen.

SEAMEN'S FUND

Together with the legislation for the supply and welfare of merchant seamen was that for the care of worn-out seamen and the widows of seamen. The Government recognized its duty to maintain a reserve of able seamen for the Navy, but it could not consider it its function to ensure more humane treatment of seamen no longer of use to the Navy. Yet at the end of the seventeenth century, a precedent was established by the Act which provided for the care of disabled seamen, their wives and children, in the Royal Naval Hospital at Chelsea. The hospital was established in 1694 for the relief of seamen injured while on duty on board ships belonging to the Crown, to provide sustenance for widows of seamen slain or disabled in such service, and for the relief and encouragement of seamen. Amending acts followed this, but as was so often the case with such acts, they were ineffective. In 1695 and 1747 a new precedent was set by " an act for the relief and support of maimed and disabled seamen, and the widows and children of such as shall be killed, slain, or drowned in the merchants service," in that it and its successor set up a body of men to supervise the collection of money from the pay of all seamen to make up a fund out of which aid should be paid.[91] The " President and Governors " had little real power since the funds were collected and handled locally in over a hundred different ports. But at least something was being done for the helpless seamen.

By the eighteen-thirties, the local administration of the funds was obviously unsatisfactory. Petitions were sent to Parliament with complaints of the inadequacy of the funds in some ports, of their poor administration, and of the generally bad lot of the sick sailor. Finally, in 1834, George Lyall, the London shipowner, who had helped reorganize Lloyd's Register of shipping, introduced a private Member's bill to amend the Act of 1747. It was largely a reiteration of the provisions of the previous act, so that there was little opposition except to one clause. All merchant seamen had always contributed sixpence a month each to the upkeep of the Chelsea Hospital, which was operated by and for the Navy; this clause abrogated that obligation and therefore the Government opposed the clause. It could not oppose the whole Act, but the First Lord of the Admiralty, Sir James Graham, and the President of the Board of Trade, Poulett Thomson, did not want to lose the £22,000 the seamen contributed to the hospital, although at the time there were no seamen in the hospital who had not been in the Navy. The Government's economical ambitions made the loss of any income unthinkable. But the injustice to the seamen of their contributing to a hospital which they did not use was apparent; the Government's objection was defeated, and the bill was passed.[92]

Although this Act of 1834 had little effect, it brought the plight of seamen out into the open, and constituted the opening wedge for further and more effective reforms. Furthermore, it did make the establishment of a separate hospital for merchant seamen necessary. *The Times*, the General Shipowners' Society and many other organizations supported it. Within a few weeks meetings were held to get it started. And the next year, in 1836, the select committee of inquiry into the causes of shipwrecks, finding that the Seamen's Fund was not adequate, recommended the establishment of savings banks for seamen and also an asylum for worn-out seamen. Petitions continued to flow in complaining of the lack of education of seamen, inadequate funds and many other grievances. To supplement the Government's rather too incomplete activity, private charities were established, like the Shipwrecked Fishermen's and Mariners' Benevolent Society. But they were inadequate. The clamour continued, so that in 1840, the Government resorted to the usual solution : it secured the appointment of a select committee of the House of Commons to inquire into the Merchant Seamen's Fund. The committee thoroughly examined the institution of the President and Governors of the Fund, and found that the hundred and more separate funds were very unequally managed, that some had almost no money, some collected their funds irregularly, some invested the funds badly, and in general, they all had too little money anyhow. Since it was not enough for the local bodies to send yearly reports to the governing body in London, the committee recommended the transference of all funds to London and, with the establishment of similar management everywhere and a uniform scale of allowances, it hoped that the reform would guarantee better insurance for all. The Governors in London were to establish various classes of urgency. The transition to the new order was eased by the provision that local authorities should continue collecting the dues and that they should advise the central board. Furthermore, although these recommendations seem mild compared to other reforms at that time, the committee felt sufficiently shy to conclude its report with the statement that because of the jealousies between seamen and their employers, or between gentlemen acting in local trusts and the corporation of London, it did not recommend immediate introduction of a bill but hoped " that when the expediency and justice of the measure are maturely considered, and when it is perceived that the suggested

T.B.T.

alteration has not originated in any distrust of the actual management, but on a conviction of the insufficiency of the existing law,
those who are interested in the funds, whether as contributors or
superintendents, will become concurring parties to the introduction of a measure in a future year founded on the suggestions of
this Report." [93]

The committee was more timid than the Government, for the
Board of Trade, as that department of the Government most
concerned with general matters of shipping, prepared a bill
incorporating the recommendations of the committee. However,
the change of ministry in September of that year, 1841, inter-
rupted any plans the Government might have had and the bill
was laid aside.

Meanwhile a private committee, appointed in 1840 by the sea-
going owners, masters and mates, and seamen of London,
continued their efforts to secure Parliamentary action. [94] With the
increasing number of bank failures, in which seamen's funds were
kept, the refusal by some of the local trustees to furnish the returns
requested by London, and the general discontent of seamen, by
1843 they were able to send a very strong memorial to the Board of
Trade, reaffirming the case for action. Gladstone, at the Board,
thereupon ordered Shaw-Lefevre, one of the joint assistant secretaries, to examine all Acts having anything to do with seamen and
to prepare a full report, including his recommendations for future
action. [95] Unfortunately, like so many of the other papers of the
Board, his report has not been found, but its contents stirred
Gladstone to action, for early in the next year, he secured the
appointment of a select committee to inquire into the Seamen's
Fund. He chaired the inquiry himself and soon the committee
reported. It recommended that all the money be paid into one
general fund, that it be collected by the customs, that the general
fund continue to be handled by the President and Governor but
that " the Board of Trade be authorized to call for accounts and
Information from the President and Governors, and from the
Trustees at the Outports, and from the persons having charge of
the financial business of the Fund . . . and also to define the Law
of Probability which may safely be applied to it, so as eventually
to calculate a Scale of Pensions, or other benefits, equivalent to
the subscription." [96] All uncertainty had gone, the attitude of the

committee was explicit. It concluded its report with the recommendation " that a Bill should be framed in accordance with these Resolutions."

Again, however, any action was frustrated. The Board of Trade introduced its bill early in the next session, but local interests proved too strong. The shipowners and others, who generally liked things as they were and were against navigating ships by act of Parliament, defeated the Government. Concerned with other controversial matters and not willing to fight for people who could not muster more support for themselves, the Government withdrew the bill. The opposition promised that it would support a more " mature proposal." [97]

The agitation continued. More memorials from seamen for reform produced a royal commission in 1847 headed by Lord Ellenborough, recent First Lord of the Admiralty under Peel, and Admiral Sir Edward Codrington, the " hero " of Navarino and long a friend of seamen. They reported that, " having fully considered the whole subject referred to us . . . , we regret that we are unable to hold out any hope that a continued adherence to the present system, or any partial amendment of it, will secure to the worn out merchant Seamen that just and adequate relief which it is the benevolent wish of Your Majesty and of Parliament to confer upon them." [98] They offered the same recommendations as the previous committee. But another three years went by before anything was done. Only in 1850, when the Government recognized the need for consolidation, were the recommendations of the various inquiries realized.

EMIGRANTS

By the late eighteen-thirties Melbourne and his Whig colleagues were tired. Their reforms had further freed business from old restraints but they had only begun to admit that a liberal economy might not necessarily benefit all people, certainly not right away. There were its victims who were unable to help themselves and therefore had to be protected by the Government. Thus the Whigs had ameliorated the lot of factory children and the chimney-sweeps, and ensured merchant seamen more humane treatment.[99] But they had overlooked a growing number of people who in some ways were the most exploited of all. Emigrants were completely at the mercy of their new masters, the ship captains.

More than 60,000 persons each year emigrated from Great Britain.[100] Some left for adventure, but the great majority left to escape starvation. A long sea voyage and an unmapped wilderness were better than that, but they understood the terrors of their adventure only after they had sailed. Forced to live aboard ship like gypsies, carry their own supplies, cook their own meals, packed in like slaves, they had little to live on but hope. Deluded into thinking that the voyage would last only three weeks and too poor to buy much food, they usually carried inadequate provisions for the eight weeks or more at sea, and to obtain their desperately needed supplies they had to buy from the captain at high prices or steal from their fellow passengers. Few ships carried enough drinking water or were constructed to allow for proper ventilation. Furthermore, ships were frequently so unseaworthy that they would not carry full sail, and wallowed along week after week only prolonging the misery of the emigrants. Medicines and surgeons were quite inadequate. Thus starvation at home was too frequently avoided by death at sea. The inspecting physician at Quebec reported that he was " at a loss for words to describe the state in which the emigrants frequently arrived; with a few exceptions, the state of the ships was quite abominable; so much so, that the harbour-master's boatmen had no difficulty at the distance of gunshot, either when the wind was favourable or in a dead calm, in distinguishing by the odour alone a crowded emigrant ship." [101]

Whereas the helpless at home remained within sight, the emigrants could protest only after arrival in the new world. They then were so involved in new problems that they could not worry about future emigrants. In any case complaints would not be read in England for many months and were easily ignored. Although some persons in England would have discouraged emigration because it meant less cheap labour and therefore higher wages, others believed it was the only solution to the grave problem of overpopulation and would decrease the risk of social disturbance. (Those were the restless years of chartism and socialism.) Yet there were the few who went beyond debating its effects and did something about its conditions. They organized charities to lend money or to give supplies to emigrants embarking, and also to secure from Parliament an act forcing shipowners and captains to meet certain standards. They had succeeded, in fact, as far back as 1803 in passing a Passenger Act.[102] Emigration was not then serious, but with most members of Parliament preoccupied, the shipping interest disorganized, and with peace, it was the right time for action. The provisions were impressive : the number of passengers was limited to one for every two tons of the burden of the ship, certain provisions were to be carried, cargoes properly stowed, muster roles submitted to the customs, a surgeon with a proper medicine chest to be carried if there were more than fifty passengers, and bedding was to be aired daily. The customs officers were given the responsibility of seeing that these provisions were carried out. But war was soon resumed; emigration and the Passenger Act were forgotten.

After 1815 emigration gradually increased, and the original Act of 1803 was supplemented by others (those applied only to emigration to British North America), but they remained significant only as statutes. Customs officers were primarily responsible for their implementation but they were too busy with their regular duties, and the Treasury was little interested. Colonial governors were given certain powers, but in practice about all they could do was write reports. After all, the problem was to improve conditions before the ship sailed; after it arrived, it was too late. The Colonial Office further accepted some responsibility by appointing a commission on emigration in 1831 which sat for only a year and did little because it held the view that direct interference of the State was not required. Nevertheless emigration agents were appointed to report on conditions, but they had little power. With the Treasury and the Colonial Office already responsible, the Board of Trade acting in its advisory capacity answered a request from the Treasury that the Board should undertake to alter the Passenger Acts with the statement that " my Lords suggest whether this question might not with propriety be submitted to the consideration of His Majesty's Secretary of State for the Home Department." [103] Thus the Board implied that the Treasury and its customs officers should not be responsible but that the Home Department should assume the duties. Meanwhile the Board advised the Treasury to raise the penalties for infringement of the Passenger Acts and to extend their provisions to emigration to the

West Indies.[104] But the confusion of responsibility for the Acts precluded their application. The emigrants continued to suffer.

Finally the stalemate was broken in 1839 when Lord Durham issued his famous report. In it he emphasized at length the awful plight of the emigrants both on board ship and on their arrival in port, and concluded his detailed description by expressing his " entire dissent " from the doctrine of entrusting the conduct of emigration to charitable committees. It should rather be under a department of the Government.[105] With the backing of this report, friends of the emigrant were now strengthened enough to force the worn-out Government to action. Since the old departments had long learned how to avoid the issue, the ministry appointed an independent board of commissioners who were to control the whole of emigration; to control the sale of waste land in the colonies, to supervise the emigration agents, and to undertake the amendment of the Passenger Acts.[106] Now with three able men, charged with complete responsibilty for all phases of emigration, able to recast the Passenger Acts, the local agents were carefully supervised, the penalties for infringement of the Acts carried out, the emigrants began to receive protection.[107] Although the Colonial Office assumed responsibility for the Commission, one of the commissioners was also assistant secretary of the Board of Trade, which meant that in practice the Board continued to act in an advisory capacity.[108]

The work of the Emigration Commissioners gradually decreased as steamships replaced sailing ships because the former were already surveyed by the Board of Trade surveyors. Finally in 1873 the Board absorbed the remnant of the Commission's duties.

COALWHIPPERS

The coal industry and shipping were long intimately connected. Before the railroads were able to offer cheap haulage to the coal producers, canals and coastal shipping were responsible for the distribution of coal. By far the greatest single area for the consumption of coal was London. Coal was shipped from the great northern coalfields of the Tyne and the Wear down the eastern coast to London, and unloaded in London by a large number of dockside labourers. Earlier in the eighteenth century they shovelled the coal from platform to platform in the hold, into the measuring vat, from which it was tipped into lighters. They were called heavers. About the middle of the century a more efficient system was instituted. The heavers filled baskets in the hold, whipped them up above the deck by means of a pulley, and then tipped the basket into the vat. From this operation they derived the name coalwhippers, current in the first half of the nineteenth century.[109]

Unfortunately for the coalwhippers, they were not really numerous until well into the eighteenth century, until it was too late to organize them into a medieval guild which would have given them status and protection. They received none of the advantages of the highly regulated and traditionally organized industries. Attempts were made to organize them, but it was too late, for individualism had become too strong. The crucial provision that the coalwhippers should all register remained voluntary, so that their employers, called crimps or undertakers, could scare them out of registering. Without an effective system of registration, any attempt to organize them was doomed. They continued to be victimized like the lowest class of city labourers and other dock and riverside workers. They suffered intermittent unemployment and wide fluctuations in wages, which were inadequate for any kind of decent living. In addition, the nature of their work made them very thirsty, so that the crimps could take further advantage of them by selling them beer at very high prices, equal to that of brandy. The coalwhippers were certainly victimized.

In 1807 one of the provisions of an act concerning the coal trade empowered the city of London to license persons to employ coal-whippers, but the attempt at alleviation failed. In 1832 Mr. Fawcas, a shipowner, started a registry for coalwhippers, but his project also was unsuccessful.[110] However, sympathy for their plight was growing, especially in the thirties. By 1843 the agitation for their help was sufficiently strong for legislative aid. A select committee sat on the bill for coalwhippers. With Gladstone, the Vice-President and real chief of the Board of Trade, in the chair, and Sir William Clay and Lord Ashley on the committee, it did not take long to agree on the provisions of the bill; nor did the bill have any difficulty in passage.[111] The interest opposed, the crimps were too clearly in the wrong to offer effective opposition. The Act set up a body of commissioners who were empowered to open a register of coalwhippers and to appoint a registrar.[112] Registration was compulsory, and a department of the Government was made responsible for the administration of the commissioners, although that department was only indirectly specified. Of the nine commissioners, four were to be appointed by the Board of Trade. It was also to approve the bylaws of the registry and thus it was given the ultimate responsibility. Since by this time the Board was operating fairly efficiently and conscientiously, the coalwhippers at last received the protection of the Government.

As early as a year after their establishment, the commissioners reported to the Board of Trade that :

> [They] have the greatest satisfaction in the full assurance and belief that the intentions of Parliament have been attained as far as possible, within the limited time of their labors, and that a very considerable improvement has already taken place in the moral condition of the great body of laborers who are employed as Coalwhippers. That they have been removed from the most degraded state of thraldom and oppression, and are now free agents to lay out their hard earnings in their own way for the benefit of their wives and families.[113]

LIFESAVING

The use of lifeboats to save persons from shipwreck originated in the seventeen-eighties. By 1803 Henry Greathead, the foremost builder, had constructed twenty-three for use in Great Britain for private patrons or for local committees. A committee of the House of Commons commended his work and gave him 100 guineas, but did not commit the Government to co-operating with the private interests. The coastguard helped when they could, but their ships and skills were not developed for lifesaving. By 1824 Sir William Hillary and two Members of Parliament, Thomas Wilson and George Hibbert, took advantage of the feeling aroused by several bad shipwrecks and organized the Royal National Institution for the Preservation of Life from Shipwreck which was to set up suitable establishments of lifeboats and apparatus on the most dangerous parts of the coasts of the United Kingdom, and to grant rewards and to give relief to widows and families of those lost in shipwreck. It established lifeboat stations of its own and co-operated with those thirty-nine already established by individuals. In its first five years the institution saved 1,446 lives.

The famous shipwreck inquiry of the House of Commons of 1836 recommended "the institution of Courts of Inquiry to examine into the circumstances of every shipwreck, with power to reward either by reimbursement of their loss of wages and effects, or by gratuities or medals of honour and distinction those officers and men who should have particularly distinguished themselves by their skill, courage or humanity, in preserving the lives and property of others, or coming to their assistance from other vessels or from the shore.[114] Like so many of the other recommendations of this committee, this was forgotten and the Government continued to ignore the problem, except that the Foreign Office did give rewards to foreign ships which saved English lives. Otherwise it was assumed that the private facilities were adequate.

By 1850 when general interest had begun to wane, the Duke of Northumberland and Prince Albert became the patrons. With their help the institution was reorganized and public interest aroused to active support. Meanwhile the Shipwrecked Fishermen's and Mariners' Royal Benevolent Society, founded in 1839 to maintain a fund for shipwrecked persons or their widows, placed nine lifeboats along the coasts. However, in 1854 it transferred its lifeboats to the Royal National Institution and concentrated all its efforts on the administration of the benevolent fund. The two organizations have since prospered and carry on their work to-day in friendly co-operation, one to save shipwrecked persons, the other to aid them afterward or to aid their families. The Marine Department of the Board of Trade co-operated after 1854 in paying rewards out of the marine fund to persons who had helped save lives.[115]

NOTES

[1] Harriet Martineau, *Autobiography* (2 vols., Boston, 1877), i, 524.

[2] The former was the Consul at Riga; the latter at Danzig. Quoted in an unpublished manuscript by P. G. Parkhurst at the Ministry of Transport and Civil Aviation.

[3] For comparative figures of the amount of shipping, see Sidney Pollard, *The Economic History of British Shipbuilding 1870-1914* (unpublished Ph.D. dissertation, University of London, 1951), p. 3. During the American Civil War, 40 per cent. of the sea-going tonnage was sunk or sold. In any case the British marine recovered the advantage with the development of the iron hull and an efficient steam engine.

⁴ *P. P.*, 1844, VIII, and BT 5, 39.

⁵ Like all generalizations, this description ignores the many exceptions; that is, the good shipowners like the East India, the Peninsular and Oriental, Cunard, and other companies.

⁶ *The Times* (London), June 10th, 1831, p. 1.

⁷ The Shipwrecked Fishermen and Mariners' Royal Benevolent Society was founded in 1839 to form " a fund for the relief of shipwrecked Mariners and Fishermen, or in the case of loss of life, for the widow and orphans." Both organizations carry on to-day.

⁸ *P. P.*, 1836, XVII.

⁹ *Ibid.*

¹⁰ *Parl. Deb.*, 3rd s., XXXVII, 182.

¹¹ BT 1, 329.

¹² Labouchere, Henry (1798-1869), Winchester and Christ Church, Oxford; a Lord of the Admiralty, 1832; Master of the Mint, Privy Councillor, and Vice-President of the Board of Trade, 1835; Under-Secretary of War and the Colonies, 1839; President of the Board of Trade, 1839-41 and 1847-52; Secretary of State for the Colonies under Lord Palmerston, 1855-58; created Baron Taunton, 1859; grandson of Sir Francis Baring; married first cousin, daughter of Sir Thomas Baring.

¹³ *Ibid.*, XXXVIII, 1222-3. The Committee of the General Shipowners' Society was prepared in case the bill had been read a second time " to exercise their utmost endeavours to prevent the adoption of such provisions as were in the bill." BT 1, 341.

¹⁴ *P. P.*, 1839, IX.

¹⁵ *Ibid.*, 1843, IX.

¹⁶ General Shipowners' Society meeting, July 12th, 1843.

¹⁷ William S. Lindsay, *History of Merchant Shipping* (4 vols., London, 1874), III, 42.

¹⁸ BT 1, 423.

¹⁹ *Ibid.*, 427.

²⁰ General Shipowners' Society Report for 1845.

²¹ 13 & 14 Vict. c. 93.

²² Its full title was " The Master, Wardens, and Assistants of the Guild, Fraternity, or Brotherhood of the Most Glorious and Undivided Trinity and of St. Clement in the Parish of Deptford Strond in the County of Kent." See Hilary P. Mead, *Trinity House* (London, n.d.).

²³ 48 Geo. III c. 104.

²⁴ BT 5, 33.

²⁵ BT 5, 41.

²⁶ *P. P.*, 1836, XXVIII.

²⁷ To be Warden is a high honour. Wellington was Warden from 1829 till his death in 1852. He lived and died in Walmer Castle, formerly the residence of the Warden. Churchill is now the Warden.

²⁸ *P. P.*, 1843, IX.

²⁹ *Parl. Deb.*, 3rd s., XXVII, 247.

³⁰ *Ibid.*, 246.

³¹ *P. P.*, 1834, XII.

³² *Ibid.*

³³ The Treasury recommended in 1830 that the lighthouses belonging to the Crown leased to Lord Braybrooke and to Thomas Coke, Esq., M.P. be renewed for twenty-one years. The tolls were to be reduced from 1 *d*. per ton

on each ship passing to $\frac{1}{4}d$. The lessees were to deliver to the Commissioners of His Majesty's Woods, Forests, and Land Revenues, annual accounts of all tolls collected, of expenditure and maintenance, to pay one moiety to the Treasury and to allow free access at all times to the lighthouses and other premises to the members of Trinity House and to attend to and carry into effect any suggestions of that corporation for the better regulation or improvement of the lights. *P. P.*, 1830, Sixth Report of the Commissioners of Woods and Forests.

34 *Parl. Deb.*, 3rd s., XXXI, 168.

35 *Ibid.*, XXXV, 141.

36 *Ibid.*, 143.

37 6 & 7 Will. IV c. 79.

38 *Parl. Deb.*, 3rd s., CVII, 215.

39 The technical development of lighthouses was slow; they had not long been effective. In order to obtain a strong light it was necessary to have a strong illumination, and then to concentrate all the rays of light upon a single point or at least on one level. Toward the end of the eighteenth century, Teulere, the engineer-in-chief for the province of Bordeaux, improved the design of silvered parabolic reflectors which defined the rays in a limited area. And by turning them, he obtained revolving lights, which in many cases were more effective than steady lights. His system was called catoptic. Meanwhile men tried to improve the dioptic system, which used lenses to refract the light rays and make them parallel to their axes. Another Frenchman, Fresnal, deserves most credit for their improvement. In fact the French were the leaders in this field. In the eighteen-forties, the Stevenson brothers made some improvements, notably one involving a combination of the two systems, using reflectors and lenses. This was essentially that in use to-day, called the holophotel system. Except for a brief period, France kept her lead. In 1850 Messrs. Chance Brothers and Company engaged the French expert Tabouret and began to make lights. They exhibited one at the Great Exhibition. Although Tabouret retired in 1853, Chance continued to make lights, and in 1854, Faraday, the scientific adviser to Trinity House, gave his opinion that the light of Chance was equal to the French. Between 1855 and 1858 Chance made over thirty lights.

40 The word "road" originally was used to mean a roadstead, that is, a sheltered piece of water near the shore where vessels might lie at anchor in safety.

41 9 & 10 Vict. c. 100. See the section on Steamship Inspection for an account of the Act.

42 Quoted in the biography of Fitzroy in *The Dictionary of National Biography*. The international scale used to indicate in logs the force of the wind was named after Beaufort.

43 Quoted in an unpublished manuscript by P. G. Parkhurst at the Ministry of Transport and Civil Aviation.

44 BT 3, 47.

45 The instruments were one marine barometer, six thermometers, four hydrometers, and one azimuth compass, all costing £11.

46 4 Geo. IV c. 41, and 6 Geo. IV c. 110.

47 *The Times* (London), January 21st, 1835, p. 2. Meanwhile, with the reorganization in 1834 of *Lloyd's Register* of shipping, shipowners who passed Lloyd's qualifications might register their ships in a national publication.

48 8 & 9 Vict. c. 89.

[49] For a brief history of tonnage measurement see *The Nautical Magazine*, February 1871, pp. 69 f.

[50] 13 Geo. III c. 74. The equation would be:

$$\text{Tonnage} = \frac{(L - 3/5\,B) \times B \times B/2}{94}$$

[51] See G. R. Porter, *The Progress of the Nation* (London, 1847), pp. 446 f.

[52] Among the members were Davies Gilbert and the scientist, Henry Kator.

[53] The person at the Admiralty who was responsible for the correspondence with the Board was its second secretary, John (later Sir) Barrow, the founder of the Royal Geographical Society.

[54] 5 & 6 Will. IV, c. 56.

[55] G. R. Porter, *The Progress of the Nation* (London, 1847), p. 319. With its many miles of inland rivers, the United States employed considerably more steamships than Great Britain; for example, in 1836 it had about 800 ships with a tonnage of 155,473.

[56] The Navy particularly encouraged the development of the propeller because the paddle-wheel was too vulnerable for warships. In fact until a good propeller was available many naval officers were firm against the use of steam for this reason.

[57] *P. P.*, 1817, VI.

[58] *P. P.*, 1831, VIII.

[59] BT 3, 28.

[60] BT 5, 46 and *P. P.*, 1839, XLVII.

[61] BT 3, 29.

[62] *P. P.*, 1843, IX, and BT 1, 423.

[63] *P. P.*, 1843, IX.

[64] 9 & 10 Vict. c. 100 and BT 1, 423.

[65] BT 3, 34.

[66] 11 & 12 Vict. c. 81.

[67] 2 & 3 Vict. c. 44 and 3 & 4 Vict. c. 36. The President of the Board was closely connected with the timber trade with the Baltic. Baltic traders were bitter against the favour given their competitors in the transatlantic trade.

[68] The first navigation school was established by Charles II in 1763 at Christ's Hospital. The Guild of Merchant Adventurers opened a navigation class at Bristol in 1738 and a school was founded by the Corporation of Hull Trinity House in 1785.

[69] Captains in the Royal Navy and the East India Company were qualified by an examining board before taking command.

[70] *P. P.*, 1836, XVII.

[71] BT 5, 48.

[72] BT 3, 30.

[73] *The Times* (London), January 27th, 1842, p. 3.

[74] BT 1, 382, 384, 385, 386, 391.

[75] *P. P.*, 1843, IX.

[76] BT 5, 52.

[77] *Ibid.*

[78] This was established in 1841 "for the purpose of establishing a more effectual superintendence and control of the surveyors' department in this Port, than could possibly be exercised by a board in London." BT 1, 427.

[79] BT 5, 52. This bill became 7 & 8 Vict. c. 112.

[80] BT 5, 54 and BT 6, 218.

[81] One of the few accounts of this solution is by P. G. Parkhurst in his "Compulsory Examination for Masters and Mates," in the British *Journal of Commerce* for January 13th, 1951.

[82] 5 & 6 Will. IV, c. 19.

[83] Impressment, according to Lord Mansfield, was a power "founded upon immemorial usage." It was the forcible taking away of seafaring men to serve against their will in the Royal Navy. Certain classes of seamen were supposed to be exempt: those over age, serving in the coastal coal trade, in the fishing fleet and so on.

[84] In the four years 1813 to 1817, 120,000 sailors were paid off. E. L. Woodward, *The Age of Reform* (Oxford, 1949), p. 261.

[85] 5 & 6, Will. IV, c. 19.

[86] 7 & 8 Vict. c. 112.

[87] BT 3, 32.

[88] *Parl. Deb.*, 3rd s., LXXVI, 446. One opponent of the bill accused the Government of trying " to navigate ships by Act of Parliament." P. 1510.

[89] 8 & 9 Vict. c. 116.

[90] BT 5, 55.

[91] 7 & 8 Will. III, c. 21, and 20 Geo. II, c. 38.

[92] 4 & 5 Will. IV c. 52.

[93] *P. P.*, 1840, XIII.

[94] BT 1, 413. The Chairman was Admiral Sir Edward Codrington.

[95] BT 5, 51.

[96] *P. P.*, 1844, VIII.

[97] *Parl. Deb.*, 3rd s., LXXXII, 381.

[98] BT 6, 220 and *P. P.*, 1847-8, XXVIII.

[99] The successful conclusion of the anti-slavery movement in 1833 released much humanitarian energy to work for the benefit of other helpless groups.

[100] This is an average. The number fluctuated from 14,891 in 1825 to 128,344 in 1842. John McCulloch, *Dictionary*, p. 927, and Fred. H. Hitchins, *The Colonial Land and Emigration Commission* (Philadelphia, 1931), Appendix 6.

[101] Sir C. P. Lucas, ed., *Lord Durham's Report on the Affairs of British North America* (3 vols., Oxford, 1912), II, 243. There is a lengthy description of conditions aboard ship, pp. 249-53. Sometimes the death rate reached 9 per cent.

[102] 43 Geo. III, c. 56.

[103] BT 5, 41.

[104] *Ibid.*, 39.

[105] Lucas, *Lord Durham's Report*, II, 254. Durham followed Wakefield, who helped write the report, in advocating controlled emigration, so that his recommendations concerning the treatment of emigrants at sea were part of those for fair treatment, all during their trip from their homes in England until they were settled on the new land.

[106] *P. P.*, 1840, XXXIII.

[107] The Passenger Act of 1842 (5 & 6 Vict. c. 107) included many elaborate provisions and formed the basis for all later legislation.

[108] J. G. Shaw-Lefevre sat from July 19th, 1841, to May 19th, 1846, although after 1843 he spent little time with the commission. Fred H. Hitchins, *The Colonial Land and Emigration Commissioners* (Philadelphia, 1931), p. 69.

[109] For description see T. S. Ashton and J. Sykes, *The Coal Industry of the Eighteenth Century* (Manchester, 1929).

[110] *The Shipping and Mercantile Gazette*, August 12th, 1841, p. 3.

[111] Clay was a wealthy shipowner who had already done much to improve the administration of the Seamen's Fund.

[112] 6 & 7 Vict. c. ci.

[113] BT 1, 444.

[114] *P. P.*, 1836, XVII.

[115] See the *Lifeboat,* the journal of the Royal National Life-boat Institution, begun in 1852. By 1850, the budget of that Institution was over £10,000.

Consolidation of the Shipping Code

IT was time for the consolidation of shipping legislation. All phases of the shipping industry had been, in one way or another, brought under the surveyance of the Government. Trinity House was given the overall supervision of the administration of pilots and lighthouses, but it was expected to co-operate closely with the Board of Trade. That department and the Admiralty shared, with considerable confusion, the responsibility for the definition of the rules of the road. The Admiralty had begun to collect meteorological information. The registration of ships and the measurement of tonnage was governed by the Treasury, the Admiralty and the Board of Trade. Parliament had limited the freedom of the shipowners to stow cargo as they liked, and it had given to the Board of Trade the responsibility for the inspection of steamships. The Board of Trade had obtained the co-operation of Trinity House in the examination of shipmasters. Parliament had continued the Admiralty's responsibility for the registration and supply of seamen. Parliament had also accepted some responsibility for the welfare of those connected with shipping : the worn-out seamen and the widows and orphans of seamen, emigrant passengers, coalwhippers, and persons shipwrecked.

By 1850, after twenty years of legislation, forty-eight statutes had been passed involving no less than nine departments of the Government in the administration of the many phases of the shipping industry. All men were agreed that Government interference was to be avoided if possible, but in fact it was found impossible and an elaborate merchant shipping code had been created. But just what that code was it was difficult to say. The contradictions between the Acts, the confusion as to who was responsible, the vagueness of many of the clauses, rendered the whole most confusing. The amount of correspondence, written by clerks in longhand and sent around by messenger, which many decisions entailed, was enough to prevent the need for any decision. Responsibility could be avoided by any department with the excuse that it was not really responsible. And the decision of the most able secretary could be subverted. Indeed there were so many acts and authorities that much of the code was inoperative. But through the haze of semi-official correspondence and confusion the role of the Board of Trade had been established. It was only a matter of time before it was recognized and defined by the appropriate legislation.

The committee of the House of Commons selected to inquire into the causes of shipwreck in 1836 had strongly recommended setting up a central marine board in London; the other in 1843 had implied that such would be necessary in time although its opinion was not so positive. Thus two of the best-known reports had taken this position, and Murray had continued to advertise the wretched state of the British marine and the need for a central board. The loss of ships remained the rallying ground of the reformers, yet only after all the individual battles for each reform had been won could the forces unite to codify all legislation.

Furthermore, by 1850 several conditions had changed. The railway mania had abated and the Government and the legislators could think of other matters. Many of the other pressing problems of the preceding years had been solved. And the struggle for free trade had been won when virtually the last of the navigation acts had been repealed in 1849. By 1850 the Government was free to concentrate on the less controversial matter of the shipping code.

By 1848 the Board of Trade itself was advocating reform. Its President, Labouchere, who had so vigorously opposed a marine board ten years earlier, now realized its necessity. Before the Select Committee on Miscellaneous Expenditure he said in answer to a question about how mercantile questions were then handled :

> They are dealt with partly by the Admiralty and partly by the Board of Trade; principally by the Board of Trade; but we have no professional assistance at the Board of Trade of our own, competent to enable us to come to a correct decision, very frequently, upon the points that arise with regard to them. In the Bill which I have adverted to I have proposed to establish a department of Mercantile Marine, composed of unpaid officers, of which the members shall be the President and Vice-

President of the Board of Trade, one of the Naval Lords of the Admiralty . . . one or two persons connected with the merchant navy, probably the Deputy Master of the Trinity House, and some one of the most competent of the Elder Brethren of the Trinity House, or some other person connected with the commercial marine. My opinion is, that a Board of that description would be most valuable in dealing with all questions that relate to the mercantile marine of the country. The want of it is very much felt.[1]

The next year Labouchere was busy with the repeal of the navigation acts, but after his success there, he felt confident enough to turn to the other aspect of shipping. It was too late in the session to accomplish anything that year, but he informed the House that he would lay certain bills before it the next session. First he intended to reform the control of lighthouses and pilotage, to give the Board of Trade close control and to reduce dues. This was not to be a reward to shipowners because he did not consider that the repeal of the navigation acts had been anything but advantageous to them. He went on to say that :

He desired now to revive this controversy no further than to say that truth, and a sense of duty, compelled him to state his opinion, founded on much inquiry, which was this, that the present state of the qualifications of the masters and the mates, the present state of the discipline of the crews, and the general condition of the mercantile navy of England, demanded the serious attention of Parliament. [He believed no one would contradict him that] . . . it was most desirable that Parliament should devote to that subject their most serious attention, with a view to considering whether some measure could not be introduced which would be calculated to put a stop to evils of an alarming magnitude—evils which, if not arrested, threatened the prosperity and welfare of that which was considered to be in England a most vital and tender point.[2]

Lord Ellenborough agreed, and endorsed Labouchere's opinion that something should be done to improve the condition of the marine. The debates on free trade had publicized the need for shipping legislation. The discipline of the crews was so bad that the whaling fishery had been lost to America. As many as 14,000 sailors deserted in one year. So Labouchere proposed to give authority to the Board of Trade, which would necessitate that it create a department of mercantile marine, with two persons who had been connected with the merchant marine attached to make sure that the shipping interest would be fairly treated. Gladstone and a few others commented on details but there was general agreement that bills would be introduced. They were tabled so that members would have a chance to study them during the recess.

With the issue of the navigation acts finally put to rest, the President of the Board of Trade was free to bring before Parliament in 1850 his bills drawn up to codify shipping legislation.[3] Early in the session his three bills were introduced : one for improving the condition of masters, mates, and seamen, and maintaining discipline in the merchant service; one for regulating the merchant seamen's fund; and the third for the regulation of the admeasurement of the tonnage and burden of the merchant shipping. Three separate bills were ordered by the House of Commons.[4] *The Times* had changed its tune; it was now entirely behind the legislation. In a leader the day after the introduction of the first of the bills, it said that the bill was an indispensable supplement to the repeal of the navigation acts. It discussed the proposed provisions of the bill and went on to say that : " To many of these proposals there will doubtless be objections enough of that plausible character which self-interest can always borrow from theory at a moment's warning." It is indeed interference but it is true of many places, and " the uneducated and the weak must be beholden to the kindly ' interference ' of their betters. If any class may be so described, it is the mercantile service of this country, and every true friend of that service will rejoice to see something done at last for its improvement and protection." [5] The opposition protested vigorously against the measures, but *The Times* continued in its report to express the prevailing sentiment. And three weeks later after much complaint by the opposition, *The Times* said in another leader that the radical shipowners and the agriculturists were opposed to all liberal measures, but it would " be a grievous thing to the public interests if the combination of the men of inconsistency with the men of sullenness should be effected and impede the progress of a more desirable reform." [6] A week later *The Times* continued to respond to the opposition.

Another leader called the opposition of G. F. Young and his friends senseless and undistinguished, and re-affirmed its opinion that the bill would hurt only the bad shipowner, not the good.[7]

While the battle went on out-of-doors, the Government realized that it would be better to withdraw the three bills and consolidate them into one. The new bill was read a first time on April 19th. When Labouchere moved its second reading, June 20th, 1850, he emphasized that the great body of the shipping interest supported the bill, and then emphasized the three main principles of the measure. They were to make compulsory the examination of masters and mates and to set up an authority which could cashier a master or mate for incapacity or delinquency proved before a competent tribunal, to stop crimpage by the establishment of public offices to engage and dismiss crews, and to improve discipline of crews and stop desertion.[8] He pointed out that this Act would only make the existing system more effective. To the objection that the bill would give too much control to the central Board of Trade sitting in London, certainly an understandable objection on the part of shipowners and others in distant outports, he replied that he had no abstract reverence for centralization, rather he wished to avoid it. He did not want the patronage and responsibility, so he proposed establishing local marine boards at ports with over 30,000 registered tons of shipping. They were to carry out the bill. Six of the twelve members of those boards would be chosen by the local shipowners, only four by the Board of Trade, and the local boards in fact would receive some of the duties now exercised by the Board of Trade. After serious debate the bill was read.

The House went into committee on July 8th. The Government gave way to the opposition on certain details but to the general objection that the bill would give the Board of Trade too much work when it was already overwhelmed with work, and that the shipping interest deserved some consideration after its defeat before free trade, Labouchere, who argued the Government's case with skill, emphasized that it was the local boards at the outports, not the central one in London which were receiving the power; and Sir William Clay, the wealthy merchant who had done so much for seamen, coalwhippers and others, speaking as the representative of the greatest port, said that the bill would

not harm the shipping interest. With the support of the better
London shipowners for it, the humanitarians, and *The Times*,
Labouchere, beating the strategic retreat from centralization, was
able to secure passage for the bill.[9]

This Act was the beginning of the process of consolidation. It
now recognized the title, Board of Trade, which " shall mean the
Committee of Her Majesty's Privy Council appointed for the
Consideration of Matters relating to Trade and Foreign Plantations," and next established the Board's general responsibility :

> The ' Board of Trade ' shall undertake the general Superinten-
> dence of Matters relating to the British Mercantile Marine, and
> shall be authorized to carry this Act into execution, and to
> enforce by legal Proceedings or by such other lawful Means
> as may seem to it expedient the Provisions of this Act and of all
> other acts and Laws relating to the British Merchant Service,
> and may also open an Account or Accounts with the Bank of
> England in the Manner and for the Purpose herein after men-
> tioned.

The Board's responsibility had long been recognized out-of-
doors, but this was the first time it was officially stated. The Board
was to appoint local boards and to supervise them, it was to receive
certain duties hitherto exercised by the Admiralty such as the
registration of seamen, it was to set up a system for the examination of masters and mates, and it was to have the power to call
for any logbooks, consular reports (to do with shipping), and to
call in for examination various officers employed by other departments of the Government which might be concerned with shipping. The local boards which it was to supervise and to which it
was to appoint certain members, were to set up shipping officers
to take over from customs officers all responsibilities to do with
seamen.[10] The Act further detailed many provisions to do with
the treatment of seamen. The importance of this Act is hard to
overemphasize, for it officially established the Board of Trade as
that department of Government responsible for all matters to do
with merchant shipping. The new responsibilities given to it by
this Act added to those it already had, by tacit agreement if not
by statute, gave it wide supervisory powers. It was responsible for
the registration and construction of ships, the qualification and

treatment of their officers and crews, it had various powers of inspection, it was to inquire into shipwrecks and the misconduct of officers, and to encourage and regulate navigational aids. It was to take another three years of legislation before its new role was to be clearly defined and the merchant shipping consolidation was complete; but the big step had at last been taken.

Labouchere immediately established the Marine Department of the Board. Thomas Farrer, who had helped prepare the bill, was brought in as an assistant-secretary of the Board and given charge of the department. He was to be assisted by two professional officers, Captain Frederick W. Beechey, R.N., and Captain (afterwards Sir) W. H. Walker. A full-time accountant, H. R. Williams, was employed.[11]

In 1851 there were four acts which further defined the responsibilities of the Board of Trade. One act reorganized the Coalwhippers' Office. A select committee of the House of Commons, with the President of the Board of Trade as chairman, had recommended some changes which were incorporated in the Act.[12] Whereas there had been nine commissioners of coalwhippers, there were now to be only five. The Board of Trade was to appoint three, the Corporation of London was to appoint one, the chairman of the Coal Factors' Society one. Since the latter was given general supervision and the responsibility for the bylaws of the " Commissioners for the Registration and Regulation of Coalwhippers in the Port of London," the Government would closely supervise. The office would keep a register and when a shipmaster wished to unload, he was to apply to the registrar, who would send a gang to the ship. A person designated by the registrar was to be paid. Although the coal trade had never been in such a distressed state, this act offered better protection to coalwhippers, and further clarified the Board of Trade's responsibility.

A second act intended " to consolidate and amend the Laws relating to the Regulation of Steam Navigation, and to the Boats and Lights to be carried by Sea-going Vessels," repealed the two previous acts concerned with steamships and made the system of inspection more thorough.[13] The Board of Trade was to appoint permanent full-time surveyors who were authorized to go aboard steam vessels at any reasonable time and to ensure that all provisions of this act were complied with. They were to inspect ships

twice a year and to send reports to the Board, which would issue
certificates, without which the customs officers were not to allow
the vessels to leave port. Specifications as to the construction and
equipment were elaborate : watertight compartments, lifeboats,
safety valves, boilers were among the items which had to meet
certain specifications. The Admiralty was to make regulations
governing running lights. All accidents were to be reported to the
Board of Trade. The Act in general clarified and made more
thorough the various safety regulations for steamships and made
inspection by the Government compulsory at least twice a year.

A third act, known as the Mercantile Marine Amendment Act,
1851, was to be construed as part of the Act of 1850.[14] It generally
clarified and made more complete the Board of Trade's control
over the local boards. If they failed to administer the seamen's
fund in a satisfactory manner, or in carrying out any of their
other duties, the Board was to take over these duties. There were
many other provisions which made those of the previous year more
stringent. For example, the Board now had the power to cancel
masters' certificates when it considered them unqualified.

The other act of the year tidied up the Merchant Seamen's
Fund.[15] It wound up the independent voluntary fund and gave
the Board full responsibility for the welfare of seamen. This
necessitated the setting up of the Finance Department in the
Board to take care of the fund. This department also collected fees
for the surveying of steamships and handled the other non-voted
funds of the Board of Trade.[16]

By now the opposition to the Government was in retreat. The
wealthy shipowner and long-time leader of the opposition, G. F.
Young, still carried on the fight but the prevailing mood had
changed. He became a pathetic figure. *The Times* was not alone
when it commented that he was " grinding away at his visionary
grievances with as much energy as ever." Embittered as he was
over the repeal of the navigation acts, he continued to resent the
extreme measures the Government was taking. *The Times*
regretted that he no longer could use that vehicle for " disseminat-
ing his nonsense," and that it could not reply to him other than to
bid him farewell.[17]

In 1852 two Acts to do with shipping were passed, one consolidating the laws relating to the carrying of passengers at sea, which

was to be carried out by the Emigration Commissioners, the other authorizing the Government to make arrangements with foreign powers for the apprehension of seamen who desert from their ships. Neither directly affected the Board of Trade. The Board of Trade's Marine Department did set up a navigation school in London, the London Seamen's School. This school was transferred to the Department of Science and Art in 1854 and later to the Privy Council in 1857. It did, however, set the precedent for the establishment of schools at other ports by other societies.

Two important Acts were passed in 1853.[18] One amalgamated the Cinque Port Pilots with those of Trinity House, further increased the responsibility of the latter, and specified the returns which were to be made to the Board of Trade from the pilotage bodies. A concession was made to shipowners, for pilots were no longer always necessary; provision was made for compelling pilotage bodies to grant competent shipmasters certificates exempting them from compulsory pilotage. The other Act put lighthouses more effectively under the supervision of the Board of Trade. The Board was to appoint persons to inspect the lighthouses of the three authorities and to supervise their funds. Furthermore, Her Majesty might fix tolls of new lighthouses by Order in Council with the advice of the Board. Thus the two main aids to navigation had been further brought under control of the Board.

After four years of amending acts, both political parties agreed in general on the provisions of the various acts. They furthermore agreed that the existing confusion demanded clarification which now could be achieved by an act of consolidation. When Cardwell, the President of the Board of Trade, introduced the two complementary bills, one to repeal previous acts and a large one to consolidate previous legislation, there was general approval.[19] His predecessors at the Board of Trade, Labouchere and Joseph Henley, had both recognized the need for these acts. In introducing the Acts, Cardwell emphasized that they were to consolidate, not to codify, that they ordered existing legislation, with certain modifications in the interests of shipowners and all concerned with shipping. The bill would repeal forty statutes ranging from one passed during the reign of Elizabeth. It would make the one thousand clauses in the various Acts legitimate and intelligible, limit their application, translate them into modern language, and, in general, rationalize all shipping legislation. Although the Act consisted of 548 clauses—a very extensive Act —there was little debate. Where there might have been room for lengthy discussion, there was none simply because the Act was a summation of all the struggle that had gone before.[20]

The Act's 548 clauses, divided into eleven parts, covered the whole range of shipping legislation. Of the 125 Acts of that year, it takes up 112 pages, one fourth of the total space in the volume of statutes. Most of the provisions repeat or clarify provisions already discussed; others amend in various ways. The first section deals with the general functions of the Board of Trade, which is given the " general Superintendence of Matters relating to Merchant Ships and Seamen." Among the various powers and responsibilities of the Board is one of particular interest :

14. The Board of Trade may from time to time, whenever it seems expedient to them so to do, appoint any Person, as an Inspector, to report to them upon the following Matters; (That is to say)

(1.) Upon the Nature and Causes of any Accident or Damage which any Ship has sustained or caused, or is alleged to have sustained or caused :

(2.) Whether the Provisions of this Act, or any Regulations made under or by virtue of this Act, have been complied with :

(3.) Whether the Hull and Machinery of any Steam Ship are sufficient and in good Condition.

15. Every such Inspector as aforesaid shall have the following Powers; (That is to say)

(1.) He may go on board any Ship, and may inspect the same or any Part thereof, or any of the Machinery, Boats, Equipments, or Articles on board thereof to which the Provisions of this Act apply, not unnecessarily detaining or delaying her from proceeding on any Voyage :

(2.) He may enter and inspect any Premises the Entry or Inspection of which appears to him to be requisite for the Purpose of the Report which he is directed to make :

(3.) He may, by Summons under his Hand, require the Attendance of all such Persons as he thinks fit to call before him and examine for such Purpose, and may require Answers or Returns to any Inquiries he thinks fit to make :

[etc.]

The second section deals with the ownership, measurement, registry and mortgaging of British ships. The third covers the examination certificates of masters and mates, the administration of the local marine board and the shipping offices, the carrying of apprentices, the hiring, paying off and wages of the crew, together with lengthy regulations concerning their treatment aboard and in port. It includes provisions for their protection at sea and for their fair trial and discipline. The fourth section deals with the prevention of accidents, the carrying of lifeboats, the rules of the road, the equipment and build of steamships, the survey of passenger ships, the discipline of passengers and the carrying of dangerous cargo. The fifth section regulates pilotage. The sixth section covers the management of lighthouses; the seventh, the administration of the Mercantile Marine Fund. This fund was to receive all dues, fees and fines administered by this Act, and was to pay all expenses of the local marine board, the surveyors, the maintenance of the lighthouse authorities, the expenses of such lifeboat stations as the Board of Trade might erect, and so on. The Board was to sanction all expense. Part eight deals with wrecks, casualties and salvage; the ninth defines the liabilities of ship-owners. Section ten provides for legal procedure. The last section includes miscellaneous provisions.

The Board of Trade was at last recognized as an executive department of the Government. It had extensive and well defined powers for the general regulation of merchant shipping.

NOTES

[1] *P. P.*, 1847-8, XVIII, Part 1.

[2] *Parl. Deb.*, 3rd s., CVII, 221 and 222. The general debate begins on p. 212.

[3] Coastal trade was not freed until 1853. After 1848, thirty foreign countries made eighty-four changes in their tariffs. During 1851-61, England signed eighteen commercial treaties; all were considered by the Board and it advised the Foreign Office.

[4] *Journals of the House of Commons,* 1850, p. 54.

[5] *The Times* (London), February 12th, 1850, p. 5.

[6] *Ibid.*, March 4th, 1850, p. 4.

[7] *Ibid.*, March 11th, 1850, p. 5.

[8] *Parl. Deb.*, 3rd s., CXII, 108.

[9] *The Times* (London), July 9th, 1850, p. 5. The Act was 13 & 14 Vict. c. 93.

[10] Members of the local boards were to be the mayor or provost and the stipendary magistrate, four members appointed by the Board of Trade from residents in the port, and six members elected by the shipowners of the port.

[11] Farrer remained head of the Marine Department until 1886 and is really responsible for its success. He was made a baron in 1893. He was a free trader and distrusted State intervention, and yet was responsible for much of the reform in commercial law. Sir Algernon West, long a Civil Servant, said this about Farrer in his *Contemporary Portraits* (New York : n.d.), p. 70 : " He set an example, happily not required in the Civil Service, of pecuniary scrupulosity. He found soon after being appointed to the Board of Trade that the interests of that department touched so many sides of life that it was almost impossible not to be charged with favouritism to ' the interests.' Consequently he sold all British investments of every character, and did not hold any during his period of office." It is redundant to say that Farrer was a model of the Civil Servant who encouraged the Government to set up a system whereby men of his ability and integrity would serve the Government. His salary was to be £800, that of his assistants, £600. BT 5, 59.

[12] 14 & 15 Vict. c. 78, and for the inquiry, *P. P.*, 1851, X.

[13] 14 & 15 Vict. c. 79. It repealed those Acts of 1846 and 1848.

[14] 14 & 15 Vict. c. 96.

[15] 14 & 15 Vict. c. 102.

[16] Voted funds were those paid to the Board from Parliament for the payment of personnel and for regular expenditure. Non-voted funds were those collected in fees by the Board of Trade itself. The Finance Department was broken off from the Marine Department and established separately in 1865 with H. R. Williams, the accountant, as its head.

[17] *The Times* (London), September 8th, 1851, p. 4.

[18] 16 & 17 Vict. c. 129 and 16 & 17 Vict. c. 131.

[19] Cardwell, Edward (1813-86), Winchester and Balliol College, Oxford; son of Liverpool merchant; Secretary to the Treasury, 1845-6; M.P. for Liverpool, 1847-52; President of the Board of Trade, 1852-5; Secretary for Ireland, 1859-61; Secretary for the Colonies, 1864-6; Secretary for War, 1868-74; created Viscount, 1874.

[20] *Parl. Deb.*, 3rd s., CXXXIII, 571. The Act was 17 & 18 Vict. c. 107. The methods by and extent to which the Board of Trade enforced this shipping code are complex and too detailed within the framework of this book. I intend to publish separately an account of these matters and their bearing on the subsequent Plimsoll agitation.

The New Board of Trade

Review

THE Board of Trade became a board of industry. In 1830 it advised the Government on tariffs and other matters of the mercantilist code. It advised on the subject of granting to new business the privilege of using a joint stock fund, and any other matters of business which no other department of the Government could handle. Its officers and secretariat numbered less than twenty. It had almost no administrative duties and functioned only as an advisory committee. Its importance had long depended upon the personality of its president. Huskisson, for example, was a valued and useful member of the Government and took the presidency only on condition that he sit in the Cabinet, which was not usual for the President. Generally little was heard from the Board and still less known about it.

By 1855 it had been transformed. It collected and published statistics. It registered joint stock companies. It administered schools of design. It was the Government's agent in the supervision of the railways. And finally it was responsible for all kinds of details in the regulation of the great merchant shipping industry. Its president continued to advise, but now he was also a most important administrator. His officers and staff now numbered almost a hundred and soon were to increase to over 140. He had become an important member of all cabinets. The modern Board of Trade had been formed.

Every year the Board was concerned with many different subjects: lighthouses, seamen's funds, steamship wrecks, railways, joint stock charters. And every year it acquired new duties. In some cases it was merely a matter of setting up an office such as that for the registration of industrial designs, an office which collected fees and ran pretty much by itself. But other times it was involved with tonnage measurement or the administration of the

schools of design, two duties which it found very troublesome and could not administer satisfactorily. It shared many duties with other departments and seldom knew clearly the limits of its own responsibilities. Most of its jobs it acquired simply because it was that branch of the Government assumed to be best acquainted with industry, and because the Government did not know what other department to turn to.

Corresponding to the *ad hoc* nature of the acquisition of its duties, the Board added men for one job after another as needed. When the business became too great for the one or two clerks already assigned, another was added. The President and the Vice-President, who constituted the committee of the Privy Council or the Board itself, held meetings during the thirties, two or three times a week as business required. They received deputations and discussed correspondence, made their decisions and gave appropriate instructions to their secretaries. During the forties, however, the business had become so persistent that meetings had to be held more often and at stated times. Gladstone and Ripon in 1841 held meetings regularly on Mondays, Wednesdays and Saturdays for passing minutes, and received deputations between twelve and three on Tuesdays, Thursdays and Fridays. Minute books of all meetings were kept, all items of discussion entered, numbered and initialled by either officer. In fact, after the early forties the administration of the department had to be regularized. All inter-office correspondence was systematized, and all semi-official or inter-departmental correspondence, of which there was a great quantity, was efficiently dispatched. The daily letters back and forth, all written out carefully in longhand with copies retained for the files, to the Treasury, Foreign Office and other departments, required an ever larger staff of clerks. In addition to the new clerks, and men added to administer certain specified jobs like the registry office for crimps, other specialists were added. In 1845 a well-paid legal assistant was appointed. The Board had long required the assistance of legal experts for the drafting of bills and advice, but now it set up its own legal department. In the same year it appointed a librarian and authorized him to establish a library of reference. And in 1847 a précis-writer was hired.

The attention paid to the Northcote-Trevelyan report on the

Civil Service did not mean that men long before 1854 were not aware of the problem of training an efficient and able staff. It was the contrast between the well-run and the badly-run offices which underlined the report. Some offices, like the War Office where recruitment of personnel depended largely on patronage with little reference to efficiency, may have been most lax, but the Board of Trade, where patronage was combined with efficiency, had to run well in order to untangle and get through the amount of business it handled. Its clerks were literate and were kept on in their employment with regular increases in salary as long as they did a good job. Many stayed until old age, all were given super-annuation or retirement allowances, and many rose out of the rank of clerk into that of assistant secretary. The reform agitation of those years, initiated by Trevelyan who, as secretary at the Treasury, was close to personnel problems, and assisted by North-cote, who had gained much administrative experience at the Board of Trade, was as much concerned with the method of handling business as with the quality of personnel. And that was a persistent problem throughout the century because of the *ad hoc* construction of the machinery of government, the result of Parliamentary government dominated by economically-minded politicians. Any kind of sweeping reorganization was impossible. The business was done, and departments like the Treasury, the Post Office, and the Board of Trade had to be efficient. The Board had the advantage over some of the older departments like the Foreign Office, concerned with well-understood business; because much of its business was new and its presidents were able to set up new departments as need arose without fear of offence against old privileges or customs.

The steady acquisition of varying duties gave the Board the constant problem of accommodation. Its solution was difficult, the Board's own rooms in Whitehall were soon too small; various offices were located in Westminster and elsewhere. More space was built as soon as it was required, but inevitably it was soon too small. Many doorkeepers and cleaning women were required intead of a few. Inter-office communication required many more messengers and long delays. This was only a reflection of the prevailing attitude toward government inherited from a previous more leisurely age.

The problems were new, the solutions various. Expedients were tried with varying success. The prejudice against the central government, against any legislative panacea, against any doctrinaire solution was too strong for any abrupt and thorough reform. It had to be done bit by bit. The need had to be shown, and the solution debated. Amendments were an accepted part of the technique of government by consent. And the construction of the machinery of government able to cope with all the problems of an industrializing society became more difficult as more people came to influence Parliament. The adaptation of the new Board of Trade was made that much more difficult because the persons it affected most, the business interests, were the most articulate and the most aware of the technique of parliamentary lobbying. Yet the very persistence of problems and the patience of Parliament in finding solutions resulted in a government appropriate to the new society and in a transformed Board of Trade.

THE DEDICATED OLIGARCHY

Many men were responsible for the transformation of the Board. Some were interested in only one reform or cause; others were forced by their office or position to undertake various reforms. James Deacon Hume was dedicated to the cause of free trade and all his considerable ability went into the drafting of a new tariff structure. J. H. Brown, who, unlike Hume, was not an officer in any government department, nevertheless succeeded in getting through his measure of reform for the registration of merchant seamen. Other men like Thomson, who was an officer of the Board for nine years, was forced to undertake all kinds of reforms whether or not he was personally interested. He was constantly forced to try to get some agreement among the proponents of a reform, and then to convince those in favour of the *status quo* that some slight change was not disastrous. So many men thought their solution alone was possible and were not easily dissuaded.

The officers of the Board were harassed from all sides. Their colleagues in the Government were often prejudiced against reform and they were always conscious of the expense of any reform for they were very worried about the deficits. They knew only too well how most reforms hurt some person or interest, and often the Government had committed itself to allowing a privilege. Furthermore, some reforms may have been necessary for the benefit of one group but were they inimical to the best interests of the whole society? On the other hand, the officers of the Board dealt most frequently with business men who were not easily put off. Individualists, conditioned in the fiercely competitive and ruthless business world, they demanded all kinds of reform persistently and vigorously. Their deputations to the Board of Trade and lobbies at Westminster were tireless. The officers of the Board had to reconcile their conflicting requests and somehow try to decide whether their requests if enacted would benefit only one group and harm others, or whether they would benefit the majority. With few traditions to guide them, constantly forced to experiment, the officers of the Board made mistakes and too often appeared to do nothing at all. Theirs was no easy job.

They had a double responsibility. They had both to accomplish specific reforms; and also to reform their office in order to improve the technique of administration. As more and more business men sat in Parliament and became officers in governmental departments, as well as cabinet ministers, they applied more and more successfully the canons of business to government. The death of the eleemosynary eighteenth-century government may have been delayed but it came closer in one department after another. Melbourne suspected change, but some of his colleagues hastened it. They had to accept more and more responsibilities, but also to spend less money. They gradually learned how to run their offices like businesses, although some were more able than others. Thomson at the Board of Trade had considerable ability and did achieve many reforms. Peel was a man of the new century and ran the Government itself as a business.

The officers of the Board were naturally quite conscious of the demands of business and of business techniques. They were usually business men or sons of business themselves.

The brilliant President of the Board of Trade during the eighteen-twenties was William Huskisson who brought the Board out of its post-war obscurity and made it an efficient, respected servant of the Government and the ally of industry. In his tariff reforms, he may have hastened the death of the old board, but he built the foundations of the new, for in creating an efficient secretariat he made the Board a useful agent of the Government to which both legislators and merchants could turn for help. It was largely to Huskisson that the new Board owed its origin.

The leading member of the Board during the thirties was Poulett Thomson. The son of a merchant, experienced in trade himself, he was, like his famous predecessor, a free trader and stout ally of industry. The representative of Manchester in the House, he was a good friend of the cotton manufacturers and merchants. He had a wide range of interests; he studied all problems concerned with industry, spoke often in the House, was a diligent member of many select committees, and in every way was the archetype of the new politician. His application to government demanded of the Board's secretariat an effort reminiscent of the days of Huskisson.

During the early forties, Gladstone was at the Board. His ability and drive were well demonstrated. A son of Liverpool and a free-trader, immensely able and hard-working, he enhanced the general prestige of the Board.

Henry Labouchere, later Baron Taunton, son of a partner of the famous merchant firm of Hope, and grandson of Sir Francis Baring, ruled over the Board just before Gladstone and during the ministry of Lord John Russell from 1847 to 1852. Although a free-trader and friend of business, he was more than just their spokesman. The assistants to the Presidents of the Board were men so dedicated to a particular reform or endeavour that they forced the Board's importance.

James Deacon Hume, after thirty-five years at the customs, went to the Board in 1824 and thereafter helped Huskisson consolidate the fifteen-hundred customs statutes into only ten. He remained at the Board for twelve years, and continued to work for freer trade. He was largely responsible for the reciprocal trade treaties of the thirties.

George Richardson Porter, having failed in business as a sugar broker, turned to statistics. It was he, Lord Auckland brought in to set up the statistical department of the Board. He was the very model of the man dedicated to one purpose. His *Progress of the Nation* is still a useful fund of information.

John MacGregor, a good friend of Hume, also had a passion

for statistics and free trade. He assisted Hume in the thirties, especially in the negotiation of treaties with foreign countries; and in the early forties he carried on the work of Porter and Hume.

Lord Dalhousie, unlike most of his colleagues, was an aristocrat of old family. Devoted to public service, he helped establish the very able administrative reputation which the Board has long enjoyed. Although his years on the railway department of the Board culminated in its abolition in 1846, his attempt to perform an impossible task was much respected. His fame as the Governor-General of India did not completely obscure his work at the Board.

The men at the Board were able. With few exceptions, they were products of the industrial community, and sympathetic to the demands of industry. Frequently they sat for the new towns and spoke for business interests in Parliament, yet they understood that their office made them responsible to the whole society, not just to one group or interest.

They knew one another and frequently were closely connected. They were relatives of other members of the Government, they went to the same schools, they belonged to the same clubs and societies, they were of the same social class, and they were of the same governmental clique. Lord Auckland, the President of the Board from 1830 to 1834, was the son of William Eden; the man who had, with William Pitt and Charles Jenkinson, first Lord Liverpool, and father of the able Prime Minister, started England on the road to freer trade. Two members of the Baring family were presidents. Alexander, later Baron Ashburton, a son of Sir Francis, was the Tory President under Peel in 1834, and Henry Labouchere was the Whig President from 1838 to 1841 and from 1847 to 1852. David Ricardo's sister married Porter, the statistician. And Porter was a protégé of Charles Knight, the famous publisher for the SDUK and the intimate friend of all political economists. Gladstone was the godson of William Ewart's father. (Ewart was largely responsible for the establishment of the schools of design.) Sir John Shaw-Lefevre, joint-secretary during the forties, started his career as secretary to Lord Stanley. Labouchere had made the grand tour as a young man with Lords Stanley, Ossington, and Wharncliffe. Bentham had helped in the election of Poulett Thomson in 1828. Most of these men went either to Trinity College, Cambridge or to Christ Church, Oxford. And most of them were active members of the Political Economy Club, and of one or more of the Statistical Societies.

Huskisson, Gladsone, and Dalhousie were the only men of great ability among them, but most were hard-working and competent.

CONCLUSION

" What was the Board of Trade for, if not to undertake the management of such matters as this? " It had trained personnel and long experience in matters of trade and industry. What other department of the Government could better handle the new business? Statistics had to be published, railways regulated, schools of design administered, joint stock companies registered, and merchant shipping supervised. During the eighteen-thirties and forties, the Board of Trade found itself involved more and more every year in trying to carry out new responsibilities. The old advisory committee of the Privy Council for all matters of trade and foreign plantations had long since lost almost all its colonial duties to the Colonial Office, and was fast losing those for the regulation of trade. Its losses, however, were more than matched by its acquisitions. It was being transformed into a board of industry. The Board's reorganization was confused; its legal position, anomalous; but its role as an active executive department of state was assured.

Industrialization forced reformation in government. An administrative machinery had to be constructed, an inspectorate organized, and personnel trained. And together with the increase of duties and personnel went the constant problem of increasing efficiency and frugality. Reform was a constant process on every level. Central government gradually displaced local in one area after another. Public Acts displaced private, equal rights to business enterprise and other activities replaced privilege and monopoly, and gradually the empirical legislators worked out the uneasy compromise necessitated by a government administering laissez faire.

The economic revolution had forced the Government to accept an administrative reformation. While the former was often painfully obvious, the process was subtle. And perhaps the department of the Government most affected by the general application to the Government of the canons of business was the Board of Trade. It accepted its many new duties almost unconsciously until by 1855 it found itself no longer a consultative committee of the Privy Council but transformed into an executive department of state.[1]

NOTE

[1] On May 10th, 1951, Mr. Langford-Holt asked the President of the Board of Trade of what persons the Board of Trade is composed; and on what date is it last recorded that it met.

SIR H. SHAWCROSS: I must apologize for the length of this answer. The Board is a Committee of the Privy Council for Trade and Foreign Plantations, appointed by an Order in Council of 23rd August, 1786. The members of that Committee appointed by that Order in Council were as follows:

The Lord Archbishop of Canterbury,
The First Lord Commissioner of the Treasury,
The First Lord Commissioner of the Admiralty,
His Majesty's Principal Secretaries of State,
The Chancellor and Under-Treasurer of the Exchequer, and
The Speaker of the House of Commons; such members of the Privy Council as hold any of the following offices, namely:
The Chancellor of the Duchy of Lancaster,
The Pay Master or Pay Masters General of His Majesty's Forces,
The Treasurer of His Majesty's Navy, and
The Master of His Majesty's Mint,
The Speaker of the House of Commons of Ireland, and such members of the Privy Council as hold office in the Kingdom of Ireland; and
Ten named persons.
The Right Hon. Lord Hawkesbury was appointed President.

The present members of the Board of Trade are the President and the holders, if members of the Privy Council, of such of the offices referred to as still exist. The last recorded meeting of the Board, as a collective entity, was on 23rd December, 1850, but I must refer the Hon. Member to the answer given by the right Hon. Gentleman—the then President of the Board of Trade—on 15th March, 1901, when he said:

"The Board of Trade does meet. The quorum consists of one person —myself."

MR. LANGFORD-HOLT: Is the right hon. and learned Gentleman aware that a predecessor of his in 1923 replied that there was no record of the Board of Trade ever having met? Can he tell the House what future is contemplated for this distinguished body?

SIR H. SHAWCROSS: I am considering the possibility of calling a meeting of the Board specially in connection with the Festival of Britain.

MR. R. V. GRIMSTON: Will the right hon. and learned Gentleman remind himself of what was said of the Board at the time of its inception, namely:

"These high officials, all agree,
Are grossly overpaid.
There never was a Board, and now
There isn't any Trade."

MR. S. SILVERMAN: Does not the reply of my right hon. and learned Friend show how old and well-established was the principle of governmental responsibility for trade, and how for over 100 years that principle was neglected by all previous Governments until the Government of 1945?

MR. BOYD-CARPENTER: Do the provisions of Clause 32 of the present Finance Bill and other recent provisions, compelling directors of offending bodies to prove their innocence apply to this Board; and, if it does, is the right hon. and learned Gentleman aware of the concern with which his answer to Question No. 36 is expected in many quarters?

MR. HENRY STRAUSS: Is the right hon. and learned Gentleman aware that the poem which has been slightly misquoted was not written at the inception of the Board but in far more recent years by Sir Alan Herbert?

Parl. Deb., 5th s., 487, 2138-9.

Appendix A

The Presidents and Vice-Presidents of the Board

Date appointed	President	Vice-President
January 1818	Frederick Robinson later Lord Goderich and Lord Ripon	Thomas Wallace
January 1823	William Huskisson	Charles Grant
September 1827	Charles Grant later Lord Glenelg	John Wilmot Horton
June 1828	William Vesey Fitzgerald later Lord Fitzgerald	Sir Thomas Lewis
February 1830	John Charles Herries	Thomas P. Courtenay
November 1830	Lord Auckland	Poulett Thomson
June 1834	Poulett Thomson	—
December 1834	Alexander Baring later Lord Ashburton	Viscount Lowther
April 1835	Poulett Thomson	Henry Labouchere
August 1839	Henry Labouchere later Lord Taunton	Richard Lalor Sheil
September 1841	Lord Ripon	W. E. Gladstone
May 1843	W. E. Gladstone	Lord Dalhousie
February 1845	Lord Dalhousie	Sir George Clerk
July 1846	Lord Clarendon	Thomas Milner-Gibson
July 1847	Henry Labouchere	Thomas Milner-Gibson
May 1848	Henry Labouchere	Lord Granville
February 1852	Joseph Henley	Lord Colchester
December 1852	Edward Cardwell later Lord Cardwell	Lord Stanley of Alderley

Appendix B

THE PERSONNEL OF THE BOARD AND THEIR SALARIES

The Establishment of the Board in 1830 consisted of the following :

	£
President at a salary of	2,000
Vice-President	2,000
Assistant Secretary	1,500
Joint Assist. Secretary	1,500
Law clerk	500
Seven clerks 100 to	437

Secretary to the President
One office keeper, one house-keeper, one doorkeeper and three messengers at about £100 each
Four men in the corn department

Total, 23 persons.

The Establishment in 1843 consisted of :

	£
President	2,000
Vice-President	nil
Two joint-secretaries	1,500
Secretary to the President	300
Registrar	510
Librarian	300
About ten clerks 90 to	500

In the corn office :

	£
Comptroller	600
Deputy Comptroller	510
Three clerks 90 to	220

	£
In the statistical department :	
Chief	800
Two assistants 260 and	360
Four clerks 90 to	310
In the railway department :	
Chief	200
(also chief of statistical dept.)	
Inspector-General	570
Law and correspondence clerk	500
Registrar	260
Clerk	90

Also an office keeper, doorkeeper, housekeeper, and five messengers at £75 to £130.

Total, about 42 persons.

The Establishment in 1855 :

	£
President	2,000
Vice-President	2,000

		£
Two joint-secretaries	each	1,750
Assistant secretary to the railways department		737
Chief of statistical department		800
Two professional members of the marine department	each	750
Registrar and librarian		650
Accountant		875
Secretary to the President		300
Three inspectors of railways	one at	950
	two at	575
Parliamentary and legal assistant, railway department		550
Assistant for railways department		337
Assistant for statistical department		500
Comptroller for corn returns		500
Deputy Comptroller		400
Six senior clerks	average each	450
Eight junior clerks	average each	400
Thirty-six other clerks	average each	140
Surveyor general marine department		357
Office keeper		200
Housekeeper		70
Twelve messengers	average each	100

Total, about 85 persons.

BT 5, 39; BT 5, 51 and *P. P.* 1855, 31.

Bibliography

OFFICIAL AND SEMI-OFFICIAL SOURCES

Board of Trade Papers at the Public Record Office

The Papers consist primarily of the minutes of the meetings of the Board together with copies of its correspondence. Some of the minutes and letters are bound in volumes and some are stored unbound in boxes. Although the collection is incomplete, the several hundred boxes and volumes include much invaluable information.

Journals of the House of Commons

These annual volumes serve to clarify the timing of a bill's passage or of a committee's appointment and sittings.

London Gazette

Parliamentary Debates and Papers

The Debates and Papers are the chief source for this history. The most informative reports of select committees of the House of Commons and royal commissions are the following:—

	Year	Vol. No.
Steamships	1817	VI
Steam Engines	1819	VIII
Lighthouses	1822	V
Steamships	1831	VIII
Lighthouses	1834	XII
Arts and Manufactures	1835	V
Pilotage *	1836	XXVIII
Shipwrecks	1836	XVII
Deck Timber	1839	IX
Free Trade	1840	V
Copyright of Designs	1840	VI
Merchant Seamen's Fund	1840	XIII
Shipwrecks	1843	IX
Coalwhippers	1843	XI
Registration of Joint Stock Companies	1843	XI
Merchant Seamen's Fund	1844	VIII
Merchant Seamen's Fund *	1847–8	XXVIII
Miscellaneous Expenditure	1847–8	XVIII
Civil Service Reform	1854	XXVII

* Royal Commissions

MISCELLANEOUS SOURCES

Peel MSS at the British Museum

This correspondence is so extensive that only the twenty odd volumes which included the letters to and from the men concerned with the

Board of Trade or with its business were examined. Comparatively little useful information was found.

Plimsoll Papers at the Bishopsgate Institute

This rather limited collection of pamphlets and letters contains little information.

Annual Register

Papers and Memoranda in the libraries of the Admiralty and of the Ministry of Transport and Civil Aviation

Dictionary of National Biography

Dod's Parliamentary Companion

Encyclopædia Britannica

UNPUBLISHED DISSERTATIONS

JEFFERYS, J. B., *Trends in Business Organization in Great Britain since 1856*, University of London (Ph.D.), 1938.

POLLARD, SIDNEY, *The Economic History of British Ship-building, 1870–1914*, University of London (Ph.D.), 1951.

CONTEMPORARY PERIODICALS

British Almanac (of The SDUK), 1828 *passim*
Companion to The Newspaper, London, 1833–36
Economist, London, 1843 *passim*
Edinburgh Review, 1803 *passim*
Journal of Design and Manufactures, London, 1849–52
Journal of The Statistical Society, London, 1839 *passim*
Lifeboat, London, 1853 *passim*
Lloyd's Register, London, 1834 *passim*
The Nautical Magazine, London, 1832 *passim*
Pamphleteer, London, 1818–28
Penny Cyclopædia, London, 1833 *passim*
Quarterly Review, London, 1809 *passim*
Railway Magazine, London, 1835 *passim*
Railway Times, London, 1837 *passim*
Shipping and Mercantile Gazette, London, 1838 *passim*
Westminster Review, London, 1824 *passim*

CURRENT PERIODICALS

American Historical Review
Bulletin of the Institute of Historical Research
Current Legal Problems
Economic History (Supplement to *The Economic Journal*)
Economic History Review
English Historical Review
History
Journal of Commerce

Journal of Economic History
Journal of Modern History
Political Quarterly
Political Science Quarterly
Transactions of the Royal Historical Society

BOOKS

ACWORTH, W. M., *The Railways of England*, London, 1889.

ADAMS, W. H. DAVENPORT, *Lighthouses and Lightships*, London, 1870.

ANDREWS, CHARLES M., *The Colonial Background of the American Revolution*, 4 vols., New Haven, 1924.

Annals of the Royal Statistical Society, 1834–1934, London, 1934.

ARMYTAGE, FRANCES, *The Free Port System in the British West Indies, 1766–1822*, New York, 1953.

ASHTON, T. S., *Economic and Social Investigations in Manchester, 1833–1933*, London, 1934.

—— and JOSEPH SYKES, *The Coal Industry of the Eighteenth Century*, Manchester, 1929.

BADHAM, CHARLES, *The Life of James Deacon Hume*, London, 1859.

BAKER, THOMAS, *A Battling Life, Chiefly in the Civil Service*, London, 1885.

BASYE, A. H., *The Lords Commissioners of Trade and Plantations . . ., 1748–1782*, New Haven, 1925.

BENTHAM, JEREMY, *Constitutional Code*, vol. 1, London, 1830.

BIDEN, CHRISTOPHER, *Naval Discipline*, London, 1830.

BIEBER, RALPH PAUL, *The Lords of Trade and Plantations, 1675–1696*, Philadelphia, 1919.

BOOTH, HENRY, *An Account of the Liverpool and Manchester Railway*, Liverpool, 1830.

BRADY, ALEXANDER, *William Huskisson and Liberal Reform*, Oxford, 1929.

BRIGGS, SIR JOHN HENRY, *Naval Administrations 1827 to 1892*, London, 1897.

BROWN, FRANK P., *South Kensington and its Art Training*, London, 1912.

BUXTON, SYDNEY, *Finance and Politics*, 2 vols., London, 1888.

CHAMIER, CAPTAIN, *Life of a Sailor*, 3 vols., London, 1839.

CHANCE, JAMES FREDERICK, *The Lighthouse Work of Sir James Chance*, London, 1902.

CHRISTIE, O. F., *The Transition from Aristocracy*, London, 1927.

CLAPHAM, J. H., *An Economic History of Modern Britain*, vol. 1, Cambridge, 1926.

CLARK, KENNETH, *The Gothic Revival*, London, 1950.

CLEVELAND-STEVENS, EDWARD, *English Railways: their Development and their Relation to the State*, London, 1915.

CLIFFORD, FREDERICK, *A History of Private Bill Legislation*, 2 vols., London, 1885.

COHEN, EMMELINE W., *The Growth of the British Civil Service, 1780–1939*, London, 1941.

COLE, SIR HENRY, *Fifty Years of Public Work*, 2 vols., London, 1884.

COOKE, COLIN A., *Corporation, Trust and Company*, Cambridge, Mass., 1951.

CORY, WILLIAM, *A Guide to Modern English History*, 2 vols., London, 1882.

CRAIG, SIR JOHN, *A History of Red Tape*, London, 1955.

CRICK, W. F., and WADSWORTH, J. E., *A Hundred Years of Joint Stock Banking*, London, 1936.

DANSON, JOHN TOWNE, *Economic and Statistical Studies, 1840–1890*, London, 1906.

DE MORGAN, AUGUSTUS, *An Essay on Probabilities . . .*, London, 1838.

DICKERSON, OLIVER MORTON, *American Colonial Government, 1696–1765*, Cleveland, 1912.

DRIVER, CECIL, *Tory Radical*, New York, 1946.

DUBOIS, ARMAND BUDINGTON, *The English Business Company after the Bubble Act, 1720–1800*, New York, 1938.

DUPIN, BARON CHARLES, *The Commercial Power of Great Britain*, 2 vols., London, 1825.

DUTTON, RALPH, *The Victorian Home*, London, 1954.

EDGELL, HARRY, *On the Duty of Lessening the Destruction of Human Life*, London, 1847.

EVANS, DANIEL, *The Life and Work of William Williams*, Llandyssui, 1939.

EVANS, GEORGE HEBERTON, JR., *British Corporation Finance, 1775–1850*, Baltimore, 1936.

FAIRBAIRN, HENRY, *A Treatise on the Political Economy of Railroads*, London, 1836.

FARRER, T. H., *The State in its Relation to Trade*, London, 1883.

FAY, C. R., *Huskisson and His Age*, London, 1951.

——, *Round About Industrial Britain, 1830–1860*, Toronto, 1952.

FINER, S. E., *The Life and Times of Sir Edwin Chadwick*, London, 1952.

FONBLANQUE, E. B., ed., *The Life and Labours of Albany Fonblanque*, London, 1874.

FRANCIS, JOHN, *A History of the English Railways*, 2 vols., London, 1851.

GALT, WILLIAM, *Railway Reform*, London, 1864.

GASH, NORMAN, *Politics in the Age of Peel*, London, 1953.

GIBBS-SMITH, C. H., *The Great Exhibition of 1851*, London, 1950.

HALÉVY, ELIE, *A History of the English People in the Nineteenth Century*, vols. I–IV, London, 1949–51.

HARPER, LAWRENCE A., *The English Navigation Laws*, New York, 1939.

HARRIS, REV. JOHN, *Britannia*, London, 1837.

HELPS, ARTHUR, *Thoughts upon Government*, London, 1872.

HERTZ, G. B., *The Manchester Politician, 1750–1912*, London, 1912.

HILL, R. L., *Toryism and the People, 1832–1846*, London, 1929.

HIRST, FRANCIS W., *Gladstone as Financier and Economist*, London, 1931.

HITCHINS, FRED. H., *The Colonial Land and Emigration Commission*, Philadelphia, 1931.

HOLE, JAMES, *National Railways*, London, 1893.

HOPKINS, THOMAS, *Great Britain for the last Forty Years*, London, 1834.

HOWARTH, O. J. R., *The British Association for the Advancement of Science*, London, 1931.

HUMPHREYS, NOEL A., ed., *Vital Statistics: Memorial Volume of Selections from the Reports and Writings of William Farr*, London, 1885.

HUNT, BISHOP CARLETON, *The Development of the Business Corporation in England, 1800–1867*, Cambridge, Mass., 1936.

HURD, ARCHIBALD, *The Merchant Navy*, London, 1921.

HYDE, FRANCIS EDWIN, *Mr. Gladstone at the Board of Trade*, London, 1934.

JACKMAN, W. T., *The Development of Transportation in Modern England*, 2 vols., Cambridge, 1916.

JEFFERY, WALTER, *A Century of our Sea Story*, London, 1900.

JENKS, LELAND HAMILTON, *The Migration of British Capital to 1875*, New York, 1938.

KEANE, M. M., *A Treatise on the Present Condition of the Merchant Service of Great Britain*, London, 1845.

KEYNES, JOHN MAYNARD, *The End of Laissez-Faire*, London, 1926.

KINGSLEY, J. DONALD, *Representative Bureaucracy*, Yellow Springs, Ohio, 1944.

KLINGENDER, F. D., *Art and the Industrial Revolution*, London, 1947.

LAMBERT, RICHARD S., *The Railway King*, London, 1934.

LARDNER, DIONYSIUS, *Railway Economy*, London, 1850.

LEE, CHARLES E., *Passenger Class Distinctions*, London, 1946.

LEWIN, HENRY GROTE, *Early British Railways*, London, 1925.

——, *The Railway Mania and its Aftermath, 1845–1852*, London, 1936.

LEWIS, R. A., *Edwin Chadwick and the Public Health Movement, 1832–1854*, London, 1952.

LINDSAY, WILLIAM S., *History of Merchant Shipping and Ancient Commerce*, 4 vols., London, 1874.

LUCAS, SIR C. P., ed., *Lord Durham's Report on the Affairs of British North America*, 3 vols., Oxford, 1912.

LUCKHURST, KENNETH W., *The Story of Exhibitions*, New York, 1951.

McCULLAGH, W. TORRENS, *Memoirs of the Right Honorable Richard Lalor Sheil*, 2 vols., London, 1855.

McCULLOCH, JOHN RAMSAY, *Dictionary of Commerce*, London, First Edition, 1833.

MACGREGOR, D. H., *Economic Thought and Policy*, Oxford, 1949.

MACGREGOR, JOHN, *Commercial Statistics*, 4 vols., London, 1847.

MARSHALL, J., *A Digest of all the Accounts . . . of the United Kingdom . . .*, London, 1833.

MARTIN, FREDERICK, *The History of Lloyd's and Marine Insurance in Great Britain*, London, 1876.

MARTINEAU, HARRIET, *Autobiography*, 2 vols., Boston, 1877.

——, *A History of the Thirty Years Peace*, 4 vols., London, 1877.

MEAD, HILARY, *Trinity House*, London [1947].

MEEKER, ROYAL, *History of Shipping Subsidies*, New York, 1905.

MORRISON, JAMES, *The Influence of English Railway Legislation on Trade and Industry*, London, 1848.

MURTON, WALTER, *Wreck Inquiries*, London, 1884.

NEF, J. U., *The Rise of the British Coal Industry*, London, 1932.

NOCK, O. S., *The Railway Engineers*, London, 1955.

PAGE, WILLIAM, *Commerce and Industry*, 2 vols., London, 1919.

PARKINSON, C. NORTHCOTE, *Trade in the Eastern Seas, 1793–1813*, Cambridge, 1937.

PEVSNER, NIKOLAUS, *Academies of Art Past and Present*, Cambridge, 1940.

——, *High Victorian Design*, London, 1951.

——, *Pioneers of Modern Design*, New York, 1949.

POLANYI, KARL, *Origins of Our Time*, London, 1945.

PORTER, G. R., *The Progress of the Nation, etc.*, London, First Edition, 1836.

RABB, REGINALD EARL, *The Role of William Eden in William Pitt's Liberal Trade Policy*, New York, 1942.

RAYNES, HAROLD E., *A History of British Insurance*, London, 1948.

REDFORD, ARTHUR, *Manchester Merchants and Foreign Trade, 1794–1858*, Manchester, 1934.

REEKS, MARGARET, *Register of the Associates and Old Students of the Royal School of Mines and History of the Royal School of Mines*, London, 1920.

ROBERTSON SCOTT, J. W., *The Day Before Yesterday*, London, 1951.

ROBBINS, LIONEL, *The Theory of Economic Policy*, London, 1952.

ROSTOW, W. W., *British Economy of the Nineteenth Century*, Oxford, 1948.

ROWLAND, JOHN, *George Stephenson*, London, 1954.

SCHUYLER, ROBERT LIVINGSTON, *The Fall of the Old Colonial System*, New York, 1945.

SCROPE, G. POULETT, *Charles Lord Sydenham*, London, 1844.

SHORTT, ADAM, *Lord Sydenham*, New York, 1926.

SMART, WILLIAM, *Economic Annals of the Nineteenth Century*, London, 1910.

SMILES, SAMUEL, *Self-Help*, London, 1859.

SMITH, HUBERT L., *The Board of Trade*, London, 1928.

SMITHERS, HENRY, *Liverpool, its Commerce, Statistics and Institutions, with a History of the Cotton Trade*, Liverpool, 1825.

SPACKMAN, WILLIAM FREDERICK, *Statistical Tables*, London, 1843.

SPARKES, JOHN C. L., *Schools of Art*, London, 1884.

SPECTOR, MARGARET MARION, *The American Department of the British Government*, New York, 1940.

STEEGMAN, JOHN, *Consort of Taste, 1830–1870*, London, 1950.

STEWART, WILLIAM, *Causes of the Explosion of Steam Engine Boilers . . .*, London, 1849.

TAPLOW, JOSEPH, *Fifty Years of Railway Life in England, Scotland and Ireland*, London, 1920.

THOMAS, J. A., *The House of Commons*, Cardiff, 1939.

THOMAS, MAURICE WALTON, *The Early Factory Legislation*, Leigh-on-Sea, 1948.

TROUP, JAMES, *Railway Reform*, 1846.

TURNER, RALPH E., *The Relations of James Silk Buckingham with the East India Company*, Pittsburgh, 1930.

URE, ANDREW, *A Dictionary of Arts, Manufactures and Mines*, New York, 1854.

VEITCH, G. S., *The Struggle for the Liverpool and Manchester Railway*, Liverpool, 1930.

WALLAS, GRAHAM, *The Life of Francis Place*, London, 1898.

WALPOLE, SPENCER, *A History of England*, 5 vols., London, 1878.

——, *The Electorate and the Legislature*, London, 1881.

WATERSTON, WILLIAM, *A Cyclopædia of Commerce*, Edinburgh, 1843.

WEST, SIR ALGERNON, *Contemporary Portraits*, London, 1920.

WILLIAMS, FREDERICK S., *Our Iron Roads*, London, 1852.

WILLIAMS, O. Cyprian, *The Historical Development of Private Bill Procedure and Standing Orders in the House of Commons*, vol. 1, London, 1948.

WOODWARD, E. L., *The Age of Reform*, Oxford, 1938.

WRIGHT, CHARLES, and PAYLE, C. EARNEST, *A History of Lloyd's*, London, 1928.

ARTICLES

BEALES, H. L., " The New Poor Law," *History*, XV (1931), 308–319.

BLADEN, V. W., " The Potteries in the Industrial Revolution," *Economic History*, I (1926), 117–130.

BREBNER, J. BARTLET, " Laissez Faire and State Intervention in Nineteenth Century Britain," *Journal of Economic History, Supplement* VIII (1948), 59–73.

BROWN, LUCY, " The Board of Trade and the Tariff Problem, 1840–2," *English Historical Review*, LXVIII (1953), 394–421.

CARR, SIR CECIL, " The Mechanics of Law-Making," *Current Legal Problems*, IV (1951), 122–136.

CLAPHAM, J. H., " The Last Years of the Navigation Acts," *English Historical Review*, XXV (1910), 480–501, 687–707.

CLARKE, MARY PATTERSON, " The Board of Trade at Work," *American Historical Review*, XVII (1912), 17–43.

HUGHES, EDWARD, " Civil Service Reform, 1853–5," *History*, XXVII (1942), 51–83.

——, " Sir Charles Trevelyan and Civil Service Reform, 1853–5," *English Historical Review*, LXIV (1949), 53–88.

LINGELBACH, ANNA LANE, " The Inception of the British Board of Trade," *American Historical Review*, XXX (1925), 701–727.

——, " William Huskisson as President of the Board of Trade," *American Historical Review*, XLIII (1938), 759–774.

LOWER, A. R. M., " From Huskisson to Peel : A Study in Mercantilism," *Essays in Modern English History*, Cambridge, Mass., 381–404.

MCGREGOR, O. R., " Civil Servants and the Civil Service : 1850–1950," *Political Quarterly*, XXII (1951), 154–163.

MATHER, R. C., " The Railways, the Electric Telegraph and Public Order during the Chartist Period, 1837–1848," *History*, XXXVIII (1953), 40–53.

NAPIER, J. B., " The History of Joint Stock and Limited Liability Companies," *A Century of Law Reform*, London, 1901.

PARKHURST, P. G., " Centenary of Mercantile Marine Department," *Journal of Commerce*, 1950.

PARKHURST, P. G., "Compulsory Examination for Masters and Men," *Journal Commerce*, 1951.

POLLINS, HAROLD, "The Finances of the Liverpool and Manchester Railway," *Economic History Review*, 2nd series, V. (1952), 90–97.

SHANNON, H. A., "The Coming of General Limited Liability," *Economic History*, II (1933), 267–291.

SORENSON, LLOYD R., "Some Classical Economists, Laissez Faire, and the Factory Acts," *Journal of Economic History*, XII (1952), 247–262.

TAYLOR, BASIL, "The Mission of an Art School," *The Listener*, January 29, 1953, 172–174.

THOMAS, J. ALAN, "The System of Registration and the Development of Party Organization, 1832–1870," *History*, XXXV (1950), 81–98.

THOMAS, M. W., "Origins of Administrative Centralization," *Current Legal Problems* (1950), 214–235.

WALKER, KENNETH O., "The Classical Economists and the Factory Acts," *Journal of Economic History*, I (1941), 168–177.

WALPOLE, K. A. "The Humanitarian Movement of the Early Nineteenth Century to Remedy Abuses on Emigrant Vessels to America," *Transactions of the Royal Historical Society*, XIV (1931), 197–224.

INDEX